THE BEGINNER'S GUIDEBOOK TO PERSONAL FINANCE AND MONEY MANAGEMENT

Learn to Manage Your Money, Open Bank Accounts, Create a Budget, Rent an Apartment, Start Investing, and Buy a Car, House and Insurance

By Mark A. Thompson

1st Edition

Cover Photo by Mark A. Thompson

Cover Photo Subject: Entrance to the Narrows Slot Canyon created by the Virgin River in Zion National Park, Utah

ISBN 9798742221562

Chapter 1: Starting from Scratch

Handling and managing your money are two of the most important things that you will do in your life. If you do them right, happiness is not guaranteed, but, if you do it wrong, misery will certainly fall upon you. This Guidebook teaches you the basic, practical things you need to know to properly handle and manage your money in the real world. You will learn how to open checking and savings accounts and create a budget. It also walks you through the major transactions that most people face in their lives. You will learn how to rent an apartment, buy a car and buy a house. This Guidebook teaches you how to start investing for retirement and to create wealth. In addition, this Guidebook teaches you how to protect your wealth with insurance. This Guidebook focuses on you as a single person but also discusses the complexity added to money management when you add another adult to your life. Read or listen to this Guidebook carefully and keep it as a reference guide to use as your financial matters get more complicated.

Unless you are one of the few fortunate people to be given a trust fund or large inheritance to spend in your life, you will need to earn your money to be able to handle and manage it. Finding the right job is outside the scope of this Guidebook, but, to get a job, you need to provide your prospective employer with proper identification documents. Generally, that means providing a driver's license or identification card issued by your state of residence and a social security card issued by the Social Security Administration. In addition, most employers will pay you electronically rather than giving you a paper paycheck or cash. That means you need to tell your employer where to send your pay. There are several options where you can have your money sent. You can open a checking account at a bank, savings bank or credit union either online or in person. You can purchase a reloadable, prepaid debit card at Walmart, Target or other major retailers who sell gift and prepaid cards. You can open an account with an online fintech, which is not a bank but which relies on a bank to hold your money. Chapter 2 discusses the advantages and disadvantages of these options.

Chapter 3 discusses budgeting. Budgeting shouldn't scare you. You already do it. It is just a formal way of stating how much you will earn and how much you will spend. If you have $20 in your pocket and want to go to the movies, a budget determines if you can do that. How much will the ticket cost? Can you buy a drink and popcorn? If the ticket is $15, then you only have $5 left for your refreshments. Better stick to water from the drinking fountain and popcorn, only if you can share the cost with a friend. That's budgeting. This Guidebook helps you design a budget built from your paycheck as the source of money and subtracting fixed monthly costs (rent, utilities, cell phone, etc.) to determine what is left for flexible spending items (food, clothes, cable, internet, etc.).

With a job, you can look at living independently from whomever is currently providing you with shelter. Generally, you start by renting an apartment, condominium or house on your own or more likely with a friend or two. Chapter 4 discusses the basic issues that you should consider when renting your shelter.

Renting also means establishing accounts with your local providers of electricity, natural gas, water, sewer, and garbage pickup. After you rent a place, you will need to contact certain utility companies, gas, electric, water and sewer, to obtain service. Chapter 5 discuss how to establish these relationships and what their requirements will be.

With a job, you also will need telephone service. Today, that generally means getting a cell phone and choosing a talk, text and data service plan. This area is one where social pressure and the desire for pleasure may lead you to unknowingly make a choice that limits your ability to reach other financial goals. Chapter 6 discusses the issues you should consider when getting a cell phone and choosing a talk, text and data service plan.

Transportation is another big money item that you also need to worry about. Will you use public transportation? Do you need a car? These matters are discussed in Chapter 7.

Borrowing and leasing are discussed in Chapter 8. These are sources of money other than paychecks. If properly handled, borrowing and leasing are not inherently bad. In fact, borrowing and leasing are useful in helping you to meet your goals in life. They are inevitable for most people if they want to buy a car or a house. It is important to understand the cost of borrowing and leasing. Credit cards are a very expensive way of borrowing money but they too are useful if properly managed.

Having savings is discussed in Chapter 9. Starting early is very important. Your savings account provides you with an emergency fund for unexpected expenses and interruptions in your employment.

Chapter 10 discusses the basic things you need to know about investing, such as, the terminology used in investments. This Guidebook describes how to start a basic investment program that will succeed. Many people fear investing but an investment program is not hard to establish and maintain successfully over the long term. It is essential to your success to have an investment program. You do not have to put a lot of money into investments but you should try to get started early in your career. You will be pleasantly surprised to watch the value of your investment account grow over time with little effort on your part. This chapter also discusses the use of tax deferred employer-sponsored retirement plans and individual retirement plans.

Buying a car is discussed in Chapter 11. It covers buying new versus used and borrowing or leasing. The full costs of owning a vehicle are reviewed to help you build a car budget.

Chapter 12 covers buying a house. It takes you through the process of buying a house from selecting a real estate broker through closing the transaction.

Chapter 13 discusses the insurance policies that you will need to purchase during your life as well as additional policies that you should purchase to help you manage financial risks in the face of the unexpected events of life. The focus is on the proper use of insurance to manage the risks incurred in living.

While you may think this Guidebook has too much for you to learn, I have tried to keep it simple, sticking to the basic things you need know while giving you hints on how to avoid common mistakes. Certain parts of this Guidebook, such as how to buy a house, can be saved to review later. Read or listen to this Guidebook carefully. Then, before you take action, go back and review the portions that discuss the action you are about to take. Once you have started taking actions, I hope you will build your confidence that you can manage your money properly.

So, let's get started.

Chapter 2: Opening Your Checking Account

When you get a job, you need to tell your employer where to send your pay. There are several options where you can have your money sent. You can open a checking account at a bank, savings bank or credit union either online or in-person. You can purchase a reloadable, prepaid debit card at Walmart, Target or other major retailers who sell gift and prepaid cards. You can open an account with an online fintech, which is not a bank but which relies on a bank to hold your money. For example, Chime is a popular application providing access to banking services. Chime is the fintech that developed the application. Chime partners with The Bancorp Bank and Stride Bank, N.A., to provide users with banking services. If you plan on investing soon, you may also want to establish your checking account and investment account at the same place. For example, Charles Schwab provides both traditional banking and investment services.

Once upon a time, a checking account provided you with a place to deposit your money in-person and a place to withdraw your money in-person or by writing a check. People visited their bank, savings bank or credit union at least once every two weeks. When people were paid on a Friday, long lines would form in bank lobbies and at drive-thru windows. Today, most checking account transactions are done electronically. Your employer sends your pay directly into your checking account. The government sends your tax refund directly into your checking account. You pay your bills electronically from your provider's website or mobile application. Money is withdrawn at ATMs (automated teller machines) instead of in-person at your bank, savings bank or credit union. While paper checks are still used in some instances, the use is quite limited. If you do not have a computer or a smart phone, you may need to use paper checks to pay your bills.

Choosing where you will establish your checking account is an extremely important decision. Once established, it is difficult and often costly to change. You should only establish your account at a place that offers the basic services you need: acceptance of electronic deposits, bill payment capabilities, both electronically and by paper check, and an ATM network where you can withdraw money in cash.

In choosing, cost should be a major consideration. Focus on several cost components. First, consider the cost to maintain the account. This is usually in the form of a monthly service charge. Providers will often waive this charge if you meet certain requirements, such as, maintaining a certain amount of money in your account at all times or having another account or loan with the provider. Next, consider transactions charges. There may be fees for each withdrawal made from the account, sometimes in the 5 to 10 cent range. There may be fees for using an ATM to withdrawal money, often $2 or $3. Third, pay particular attention to the overdraft charges and policies. These are the charges imposed on you when the amount of a withdrawal exceeds the amount money that you have in your account, which is called the "balance" in your account. These charges may be $25 or $45 per item that exceeds your balance. For prepaid cards, there may be charges to load (deposit) money on your card, charges for each purchase transaction, each money withdrawal transaction, and charges for not using the card, that is, inactivity or "dormancy" fees.

Competition for your business is fierce. If you have a good paying job and have had no financial difficulties in the past, you should be able to find a suitable checking account that free of regular monthly charges. Some providers will even give you money upfront to set up an account with them. If you have had financial difficulties in the past, these difficulties will negatively affect your credit score, sometimes called your FICO® score, and result in you not being approved for your checking account or related credit card.

Safety of your money on deposit is also another consideration. Banks, savings banks and credit unions are insured by entities created by the Federal government, the Federal Deposit Insurance Corporation (FDIC) or National Credit Union Administration

(NCUA), up to a certain dollar amount. Currently, bank accounts are insured up to $250,000 per depositor. If the bank, savings bank or credit union fails, that is, goes bankrupt, while holding your money, you will be paid by either the FDIC or the NCUA. The funds held on deposit in prepaid cards are usually insured because the money is held in a bank that has entered into a contractual arrangement with the card issuer. The same is true of deposits held by most online fintechs. For example, Chime has partnered with The Bancorp Bank, whose deposits are FDIC insured. You should read the account disclosures carefully, however, to determine if your funds are insured. These arrangements will generally provide you with FDIC insurance protection once your funds are received by the sponsoring bank. Your funds in process, that is, your funds that are being transferred by the card issuer or fintech from you or your employer to the sponsoring bank, are not insured by the FDIC. If the card issuer or fintech fails while these transfers are in process, you may lose your money. In some cases, you may still recover if the funds are held in trust by the card issuer or fintech that is licensed by a state agency as a money transmitter or similar regulated entity. Prepaid cardholders must also worry about the physical loss of the card. While the card is usually just an access device and no funds are actually held on the card, replacing the card may be time consuming and costly. If the card has not been registered with the issuer, as is often the case with gift cards, loss of the card means that your funds are also lost.

Convenience and ease of use is another important consideration. Banks, savings banks and credit unions usually provide physically locations where you can go to deposit your money and make withdrawals. Many have multiple locations. With these providers, you can speak to someone face-to-face to get answers to your questions and ask for assistance and advice. These institutions have onsite ATMs that provide 24-hour service for both withdrawal of cash and deposit of checks. Often these institutions participate in ATM networks with numerous locations where you can withdraw money for no fees if you stay within the network. You cannot,

9

however, deposit checks at ATMs not owned by your institution. Fees, often $2 to $5 per transaction, may be charged by the providers of out-of-network ATMs and your provider may also charge you $1 or $2 per transaction for using an out-of-network provider. The major banks, savings banks and credit unions have built easy-to-use websites or applications that allow you to pay your bills or make transfers to other people online. If you don't have a computer or smart phone, accounts at banks, savings banks and credit unions will normally include the ability to write paper checks against your account that you can send to billers. Prepaid cards are convenient to load electronically and may have networks to load in person. Bill payment can be difficult. You might have to withdraw cash at an ATM using the card and then purchase money orders to pay your bills at $1 to $2 per money. The online and mobile applications that the best-of-class online fintech companies have built are often superior to those of the major banks in terms of convenience and ease of use. That is the primary competitive advantage these companies have to attract customers. Their primary weakness is the inability to deposit and withdraw in-person and the inability to speak to someone in-person if a problem arises.

Most people start with a basic checking account at a bank, savings bank or credit union. Banks are generally less consumer oriented than savings banks or credit unions. The bread and butter clients of banks are businesses. Banks have the largest footprint, with a few having locations throughout the United States. Savings banks were established to provide mortgage loans to home owners and thus focus on serving consumers rather than businesses. Credit unions are very consumer-oriented. These institutions are mutuals, that is, they are owned by the depositors and the borrowers. They are not profit oriented so they usually offer the lowest fees on checking accounts and lowest rates on loans. Most credit unions, however, have few physical locations.

As your financial needs grow and you become more informed as to your greatest needs, you may start to use different account providers, either to supplement your original checking account or as a substitute provider. Most online fintech providers, such as PayPal and Cash App, provide an option to fund your online account from your checking account. Thus, you can use both providers. Annually, you should evaluate whether your provider is still meeting your needs. It may have closed locations, changed policies and increased fees charged to you. You may have moved and your provider is no longer close to you. Do not be afraid to change to save money. Changing providers can be a hassle but will be worth it in the long run.

Overdrafts, and the fees associated with them, are a major reason people close their bank checking accounts or, in many cases, their bank closes their accounts. Unless you maintain several thousands of dollars extra in your account, overdrafts can easily occur to even the most diligent people. For example, the deposit you were expecting electronically was not posted to your account when you thought it would be or you returned goods to a merchant who did not send the refund promptly. Sometimes, your debit card transaction will be approved offline, meaning the system did not verify that you had funds in your account to cover the purchase. When the merchant processes the transaction later online and, if you do not have sufficient funds in your checking account, your provider will charge you an overdraft fee, even if it rejects the transaction. If you are married and using a joint checking account, that is, an account that both of you can debit or write checks on, you may lose track, or have no knowledge, of all the activity in your account until the overdraft notice is received. For your convenience, you may authorize a biller to make an automatic withdrawal from your checking account to pay its bill every month. These withdrawals will be processed even if you do not have the funds to cover them and can create multiple overdrafts. Once you overdraw, the provider's fees may trigger multiple overdrafts of other debits and checks. The provider always takes its fees out before paying your withdrawals.

Account providers often provide a service called "overdraft protection". Most often this involves linking a credit card issued by the provider to your checking account so your overdrafts are funded by money advances charged to the credit card. While this may seem like a great idea, and it is when your checks are not returned for nonsufficient funds to the biller or merchant, in most cases the account provider still charges a large fee per item and you also will be charged interest on your credit card balance. Some online fintechs try the hardest to solve the overdraft problem for their account holders. Bottom line here is read the overdraft terms for your account carefully so you know what will happen because it will happen to you; it happens to everyone. The best strategy to avoid overdrafts is to build up a reserve balance of a few thousand dollars in your checking account to cover any unexpected charges.

Once you have decided where to open an account, if you have chosen one with a physical location, you go into the bank and ask to open a new account. You will then meet with an account representative. You will have to fill out a short application providing your personal identifying information. You will also be asked to provide the names of one or two references so bring two names with you along with their contact information. The account representative will verify your identity by viewing your driver's license or your identification card issued by your state of residence and your social security card issued by the Social Security Administration so bring those documents with you. Listen carefully to the account representative and read the basic materials provided. The account disclosures may be contained in a booklet with dozens of pages. You do not need to read every word. Focus on understanding the charges and fees and its overdraft program. Open only the checking account that you need. Don't open multiple accounts. The account representative will usually try to sell you on more than what you want or need. Stick to the basics. Multiple accounts leads to confusion and overdrafts. Note, however, you probably will need to apply for a credit card to get the overdraft protection. Ask what happens if you don't get approved for the credit card. Can you close the checking account without any fees? Believe it or not, some banks now charge you to close your account.

Once you have opened your checking account, you will need to monitor it frequently to avoid overdrafts. Every month your provider will make an account statement available to you that summarizes the activity in your checking account. It shows deposits, ATM, debit card and check withdrawals and any fees charged. In the past, the account holder balanced his or her check register (a manual list of all transactions created by the account holder) against the account statement to see if the provider or the account holder's records contained mistakes. Today, since most transactions are electronic and financial institutions rarely make transactional mistakes, your time is better spent by reviewing the statement for any unauthorized transactions, that is, electronic debits made to your account without your permission, and fees charged. In the next chapter, I discuss budgeting. On a monthly basis, you want to compare the deposits and withdrawals on the account statement to your budget and note any differences between what you thought you would spend and what you actually spent.

Writing a check is a simple process. Your provider will supply you with preprinted blank checks that are contain in pads and sequentially numbered. To write a check, remove one of the preprinted blank checks and fill it in as follows. In the upper right hand corner, you fill in today's date. On the next line, after the words "Payable to", you fill in the name of the person or company that you are paying with the check. To the right of that space will be a "$". After the "$", fill in the amount of the check in numbers using two decimal places, such as, $134.45. On the next line will be a long blank followed by the word "Dollars". In that space, you write out the amount in words, such as, One hundred thirty-four and 45/100-------Dollars. Fill in any blank space between your words and the preprinted "Dollars" with a line to prevent anyone from adding information to that line. Finally, on the blank in the lower right hand corner, you sign your name. Once, you have signed your name, the check is ready to deliver to the person you are paying.

Depositing a check is also a simple process. With your preprinted checks, you will receive "deposit slips". These are preprinted white pieces of paper. On the right side of the deposit slip will be a place to list the cash and checks that you are depositing. There will also be a place to indicate whether you want cash back and how much. You add up the deposited items and subtract the amount of cash you want back and the net amount is your deposit. You have to sign the deposit slip if you are getting cash back. Once you have filled out the deposit slip, you will need to endorse any checks being deposited. To endorse a check, you turn the check over and sign your name in the place indicated on the back of the check. You then take the deposit slip and the deposited items to a bank teller to complete your transaction. If you only have one or two checks to deposit, most banks allow you to skip the deposit slip and go directly to the bank teller. You then insert your ATM/debit card into an electronic device at the teller station and follow the instructions given by the device and the teller to complete your deposit.

Many banks now allow people to make deposits using their mobile applications. To do this, you open the mobile application and follow the instructions. You enter the amount of the check to be deposited and then you will be asked to take photographs using your smart phone of the front and back of the check. Be sure to endorse the back of the check before taking the picture. The bank may tell you to endorse the check in a special way. Do not follow those instructions. Just write "For Deposit Only" and then sign your name. The bank may also tell you to destroy the check deposited. Again, do not follow those instructions. Instead, write on the front of the check in small letters the initials of the bank where you are depositing the checks. When you receive your next bank statement and have verified that the deposit was processed, then you can destroy the check. If your bank has not processed the deposit, you will still have the check and can take the check to a physical location to make the deposit. If you have an account at another provider, this procedure will also allow you to deposit unprocessed checks at your other provider.

Helpful Hints

Since you are beginner, I would recommend that you start with one of the larger banks that is nearest to you. Chase, Bank of America and Wells Fargo are the largest banks in the United States. That way you can talk to someone if you encounter a problem or don't understand something. Employees are normally quite willing to help teach beginners. Make sure your provider has a convenient physical location and conveniently located ATMs for your use without fees. It should offer you a no or low fee checking account with overdraft protection. If you want to use an online bank, try Charles Schwab Bank. I have used it for years. It also has an excellent, online brokerage firm to handle your investments.

Apply for the bank's credit card that is used for the overdraft protection. Do no open any other accounts. You can always add additional services later.

Your provider should provide you with free bill payment services online and through a mobile application. The major banks' mobile applications all have five-star ratings in the Apple® Store so you do not need to review their applications.

To avoid overdrafts, build up a reserve fund in your checking account. Do not let the institution talk you into doing it in a separate savings account. The interest the institution pays on the savings account balance is so low that it is not worth the extra trouble caused by having to manage multiple accounts.

To avoid overdrafts, do not authorize anyone to make automatic withdrawals from your checking account. Use your provider's bill payment system to schedule your payments only when you authorize them each month. Limit your use the debit and credit cards the bank will provide you. Use the ATM card to get cash for your day-to-day use. Make small purchases with cash. Use the debit and credit cards only in emergencies.

15

Chapter 3: Budgeting

Budgeting is a method of planning how to spend the money you have or will have. Your budget will tell you how much of each paycheck should be spent on what. Because bank statements are issued monthly and most recurring payments, like rent and utility bills, are due monthly, most formal budgets are done on a monthly basis. This allows people to compare what they budgeted to what they actually spent during each monthly period. Adjustments are then made to correct for budgeted amounts that are too high or too low. If you are living paycheck-to-paycheck like a lot of other people, you may have to compare your budget to your actual expense more frequently. Your budget will help you plan ahead so you will have enough money to cover upcoming bills.

To create a monthly budget, you first calculate what your net earnings will be for one month. Use net earnings since the tax withheld from your paycheck is not available for you to spend on other things. If amounts are deducted from your earnings besides taxes, such as health or dental insurance premiums, do not double count those amounts as expenses in your budget. Write the net earnings amount on a sheet a paper after the label "net earnings". Next, you list recurring expenses, that is, expenses that happen every month. These include your rent or mortgage payment, your electric bill, your natural gas bill, your water and sewer bill, your car payment, your cable bill and your cell phone bill. If you have credit card or other debt, you will also need to make a payment on these debts every month. Next, you list priority discretionary expenses. These are expenses that you have every month but you have discretion in the total amount spent. Food is an example of such an expense. Clothes would be another example. Finally, you list expenses that are mostly discretionary, such as, buying a lottery ticket or popcorn at the movies. Add up all listed expenses and deduct the total amount from your net earnings for the month. The result should be a positive number, that is, your net earnings should exceed the amount of your planned expenses. If the result is negative amount, then you need to reduce your discretionary expenses until you get the net result to be a positive amount.

If you are a college student, you should include in your net earnings, the amount of student loans or grants received each month. After you complete your school, your loan payments will be included as recurring expenses.

If you cannot reduce your discretionary expenses enough so your net result is a positive number, then you need to either find a way to generate more income, such as by taking a second job, or find some way to reduce your recurring expenses, such as getting a roommate to help pay your rent, cancelling your cable or selling your car.

Once you have constructed your monthly budget, then use it to make your spending decisions. If you are just starting out, then you use your budget to decide how much you can spend on a place to live, on transportation, on cable and on a cell phone. If you have already committed for those expenses, you use your budget to plan your discretionary expenses. How much do you have to spend on food this month? Can you buy those new shoes?

At the end of each month, compare your actual expenses with your budgeted expenses to determine how well you have done. Adjust your budget for the next month if your budgeted amounts are inaccurate. After a few months of comparisons, your budget should be fairly accurate in forecasting recurring expenses and priority discretionary expenses and not require any major revisions. If one of your recurring expenses changes, such as an increase in your rent, then revise your budget.

If your bank provides you with bill payment services, it will usually provide you with summaries of your expenses too. You can use this information to fine tune your budget. Some account providers may include a budgeting application with their bill payment application. Use these applications if you find them helpful, but the simple budgeting process described above, using single sheet of paper each month should work for you.

17

There are applications, such as Quicken, to budget and track every single income and expense item that you have. For most people, these applications require too much time and effort for the benefit they provide. Unless you really enjoy the accounting work, I recommend against using one of these applications. You will hate it and avoid doing it. Keep it simple. The amount of money that you have each month that is discretionary is usually small enough that you are better off focusing your time and effort on deciding the best way to spend or save that money.

With your budget created, you also need to focus on what accountants call your "cash flow" issues. You need to make sure that, when you pay your bills each month, you have enough money in your checking account to pay those bills. You are probably paid every two weeks. Your rent is probably due on the first of each month, Your electric and gas bills may be due on the 10th of each month. The car payment may be due on the 20th of each month. Managing your cash flow means you have to determine how much out of each paycheck goes to pay which budgeted item each month.

Landlords are very aware of cash flow issues that their tenants have. That is why they make you pay at least one month's rent before you can move in. This allows you to save up during the month so you can pay the next month's rent in advance on the 1st day of the next month. Utility companies require security deposits to start service for the same reason.

Managing your cash flow may seem scary at first, but if you have created a budget and use it, then you should not have much trouble making your monthly payments. After a few months, you will learn when to pay each bill so that it does not overdraw your bank account and you do not incur late payment charges. Establish a routine, stay within your budget, and pay each bill at the same time each month. If you happen to make a mistake and do incur a late charge, contact the biller. They usually will waive a few charges if they know you are trying to keep to a budget and establish your routine.

Focus your cash flow planning on those bills with the big late payment charges. Always pay your rent or mortgage payment on time. Late charges are often as much as 5% of the payment due! Credit card companies usually have a minimum late payment charge, which is often $25, no matter what amount is due. If you find you do not have enough money to pay everyone, delay payment of bills that do not have late charges, like most doctor and dentist bills. You can usually delay paying gas and electric bills for a week or so beyond the due date.

Do not make a payment unless you have enough in your checking account to cover it. Your bank will charge you $25 to 45 per overdraft item. Unless you have overdraft protection on your checking account, your provider does not have to pay the overdraft item and can return it to your biller. If you do not have overdraft protection, you can expect that your provider will not pay the item and will return it to your biller. Your biller then will charge you a returned check fee plus the late payment fee. Your biller also has the right to reprocess a returned item once. This means your biller can try again to see if the item will be paid. If your account is still overdrawn, you will again be charged overdraft fees by your provider and biller.

Mismanaging your money will have a negative impact on your credit or FICO® score. A low score can result in denial of banking services, credit cards, car loans and even rental units. Even if you aren't denied services or credit, you may have to pay more, increase your security deposit or pay a higher interest rate on your loan because you have a low credit score. Some insurance companies will even charge you higher premiums. Therefore, it is very important to keep on top of your budget and your checking account.

If you are married, handling your checking account and budgeting becomes more challenging and will require some difficult conversations with your partner. To avoid overdrafts and unpaid bills, you should develop your budget together so you both agree in advance on how discretionary spending will be handled. If you have enough money, you might consider budgeting for a "slush fund" for each partner each month. Each partner can spend his or her "slush fund" as he or she pleases. It generally works best if one of you is designated to monitor the checking account, pay the bills and manage your cash flow. Your monthly budget comparison with your checking account statemen should be done together so that you are both responsible for staying within budget. You should agree monthly on changes that need to be made if your household is having trouble keeping expenses within the budget. Money troubles are a frequent cause of marital problems so issues should be addressed and corrected early.

Often, couples can't make a single checking account and budget work. If you are one of these couples, I suggest that you each have your own checking account and budget. In effect, you treat each other as roommates for financial purposes. How much each of you will contribute to common expenses must be discussed and agreed upon. If your two incomes are not equal, it might make sense for each of you to contribute to common expenses in the same ratio that your income is to the total income of the household. Thus, if one of you earns $60,000 a year and the other earns $40,000 a year, the person earning $60,000 a year pays 60% of the common expenses (60,000/60,000+40,000) and the other person contributes 40%. This situation is not ideal, but, for some, it is a more workable solution. You may also find it helpful to work with a financial advisor (or marital counselor) to help you through these issues.

Helpful Hints

You should keep your budget simple enough that you will use it every month.

Initially, look frequently online to determine what your checking account balance is before you pay a bill.

Don't allow automatic withdrawals from your account. Manually enter the payment amount for each bill on the bill payment system. Use the calendar functions to give you alerts when items need to be paid. Do not schedule payments in advance; that results in an automatic payment.

Chapter 4: Renting an Apartment, Condominium or House

Renting an apartment, condominium or house as your residence is one of the big actions that you will take in your life. Rent makes up a huge amount of your budget, often 40% or more of your net earnings every month. Where you live affects numerous other parts of your budget, such as transportation costs, food costs and amounts to be spent on furnishing your residence. It also affects your quality of life and who many of your friends and acquaintances will be. Thus, you should spend a lot of time and effort in taking this action.

Let's begin with understanding the terminology used. An "apartment" is a dwelling unit located in a multi-unit building. Most of the time the building has been constructed specifically for apartments. Sometimes, a large house that was originally designed for a single family is divided up into individual units. The apartment building is owned by the landlord, who rents out the apartments to individuals. An apartment is usually on one level of the building. It includes sleeping space, living space, cooking space and a bathroom. A studio apartment has two rooms, the bathroom and the other room. The other room is used for sleeping, living and cooking. A one-bedroom apartment has three rooms: the bathroom, the bedroom and a large room, which generally combines a living room, dining room and kitchen area. A two-bedroom apartment has four rooms, the bathroom, two bedrooms and a large room, which combines a living room, dining room and kitchen area. Sometimes, a two-bedroom will also have two bathrooms. An apartment may be rented unfurnished or furnished. An unfurnished apartment does not include any furnishings at all, but it will come with some appliances, such as a stove, a refrigerator and sometimes dishwasher or a washer/dryer. A furnished apartment includes a sofa, one or two living room chairs, a dining table and a few chairs, and a bed for each bedroom. The extent and quality of the furnishings will vary so you have to carefully check out what you get. Apartment buildings or complexes often will have a manager and full time staff that handle the rentals and maintenance of the building.

A "condominium" (condo) usually looks like an apartment. The ownership structure, however, differs from an apartment. Each condominium in a building may have a different owner. The building itself, the walls, the lobby and other common areas, are owned by a condominium association, which, in turn, is owned partially by each of the condominium unit owners. In contrast to an apartment building, where every unit is rented, a condominium building includes units where the owner lives as well as units that have been rented to others. In some cities, you also have what are called "coops" or "cooperative housing". In a coop, the building is owned by a cooperative association, which is owned by all the residents of the building. The individual living spaces are permanently leased to individual residents by the cooperative association. In leasing a condominium unit or coop, you must get agreement and approval from both the unit owner/occupant and the association.

A "house" is a separate structure designed for one family to live in. If it is designed for two families to live in separately, it is called a duplex. A house consists of multiple rooms: a living room, kitchen, one or more bedrooms and bathrooms. The house may be one or two stories, with or without a basement, and with or without a garage. With a house, you normally get use of the yard surrounding the house. A "townhouse" is usually at least two stories with the side walls attached to the adjacent townhouses. Each townhouse in a development is individually owned with a commonly-owned association to handle maintenance and repairs to common elements.

When you rent your residence, you will be required to sign a "lease". The lease is the legal agreement that specifies what you are renting, how long you will be entitled to live there, how much you will pay to stay there and what happens if you do not do what you promise. You are called the "tenant" or "lessee". The person or company that you rent from is called the "landlord" or "lessor". The printed terms of a lease are rarely negotiable. Most states have a landlord/tenant law that limits what the landlord can require of you and imposes certain minimum duties that the landlord has to every tenant. You negotiate the monthly rent, the term of the lease (how long you stay there) and a few other items, such as parking rights. Besides the monthly rent, which is payable in advance, landlords usually require you to pay in advance a security deposit, which is usually equal to one month's rent, and the last month's rent. Thus, you are normally required to pay an amount equal to three months' rent at the time you sign the lease. In addition, the landlord may impose other charges, such as, an application fee, a credit check fee, a fee for keys, a move-in fee, a monthly parking fee and a fee for common expenses and maintenance. Read the lease and other documents carefully so that you understand what you have to pay upfront and monthly and which amounts are nonrefundable. Pay attention to when rent is due, when payment will be considered late and what the penalty will be if you pay late. It is common for the late payment penalty to be as much as 5% of the amount of the rent due. Some charges may be imposed when you move out, such as a cleaning fee or painting cost. Security deposits are held by the landlord to pay for any damages you cause to the residence. If you cause no damages, then the amount is refunded to you, usually within 30 or 60 days after the lease ends. Some utility costs, such as water and sewer, may be included in your rent and will be paid by the landlord. Other utility costs, such as electric, gas, cable and landline telephone, are usually paid by the tenant.

Use your budget to determine how much you can afford for monthly rent. A rule of thumb is 30 to 40% of your net earnings. Include in your rental amount all of the recurring fees you will charged by the landlord, such as monthly parking fees. Do not include utility costs for electric, gas, cable, water and sewer. Determine how you will pay the first month's rent and the upfront deposits, that is, the security deposit and last month's rent. Estimate

23

other amounts you will need upfront to rent your residence, such as security deposits for utilities, utility installation charges, furnishings, dishes, pots and pans, bedding and even the shower curtain. Remember to include moving costs if you have to pay someone to move you. Save up money to pay those upfront expenses or arrange to borrow the money from someone. If you are in a large city, you can also rent furnishings. Furniture rental is a bit expensive, but, if you are short of cash or only leasing for a short time period, it may be a good service for you.

Once you have the funds arranged to pay the upfront costs, you can begin your search for a rental that is within your budget. If you cannot afford to pay all the upfront costs, you can still search for a rental, but you need to look for rentals with no or limited upfront costs. Rentals with no or limited upfront costs, include sharing arrangements where you rent a room from the owner of the residence or rent a bedroom in a two-bedroom apartment that is already rented to someone else. You can also team up with one or more friends, who do have money, to look for an apartment together. In addition, not all landlords require a security deposit and first month's and last month's rent. Some, usually in older, small buildings or houses, may only require a small security deposit and first month's rent.

In searching, it is best to take along a parent or friend to help you. There is a lot to consider and having an experienced advisor along can really help you avoid making serious mistakes. It is easy to get caught up in the moment, miss important things and make bad choices. It can also be overwhelming to consider all the important items. It is helpful if your companion can drive while you look to see what is around the rental property, the condition of the neighborhood, the availability of a grocery store and other shops and access to public transportation. You should listen to the noise levels in the neighborhood.

When you find a rental that you like, try to look at the actual unit you will be living in if you can. Often, it is rented out and you can only see diagrams of the floor plan and pictures of the unit or similar units. If it is rented, find out when it becomes available. Discuss with landlord or manager what is required to be approved as a tenant, such as, the application and credit review process. Understand the fees, what is and isn't refundable. Understand how much the rent is, what is included in that amount and what extra fees there are, such as parking fees. Decide on the term of the lease. Normally, leases are for a year, but often landlords will rent for shorter periods of time. The rent may be higher for shorter term leases than for a one-year lease.

Renting a condominium or coop is similar to renting an apartment. Just a few more steps are involved. In addition, to making the agreement with the owner of the condominium or coop, you must be approved by the board of directors of the condominium or coop association. This will likely involve additional forms, fees, delay and uncertainty. With a condominium or coop, you should ask about the ability to renew your lease when the original term is over. Unlike the apartment owner, the condominium or coop owner may only want to lease the unit for a short term. The owner may be selling the unit and your rental is just to fill the gap. You do not want to be surprised when you are asked to move out at the end of the original lease term. Condominiums and coops always have a monthly charge called the common area maintenance fee. This charge can be substantial and may increase during the term of your lease so make sure you understand whether you or the owner will be paying this fee. The other condominium or coop owners often feel burdened by owners who rent. There may be special fees for renters and move-in and move-out times may be restricted to weekdays, 10 am to 4 pm. You may have to reserve an elevator to move in and out and pay an extra fee for that. You may also be required to pay an additional security deposit to the condominium or coop association to cover damages to common areas and the elevator during your move in and out. On a more positive side, condominium or coop owners often include some nice furnishings with the unit and kitchens may come fully stocked with dishes, glassware, pots and pans. Condominiums usually come with in-unit dishwashers and washer/dryers.

Renting a house follows the same leasing process as an apartment. Maintenance and repairs should be thoroughly discussed. You may be required to mow the grass, rake the leaves and shovel the snow. Major repairs should be the owner's responsibility, but you may be responsible for minor repairs, like leaky faucets and changing light bulbs.

After you make your decision, contact the landlord or manager and fill out the paperwork and start planning for your move in. The landlord or manager will let you know when you are approved. If you are renting a condominium or coop, remember to get association approval, too. If approved, then, you will need to get your funds together and sign the lease. The landlord or manager will usually walk you through their move-in procedure, what day you can move in and what hours you can do the move in. They can also tell you what companies to contact for your utilities.

If you are sharing your residence with someone else, you should screen that person carefully. If you both sign the lease, you will be responsible for paying everything if you co-tenant does not pay. Think about your lifestyles. Are you compatible or will you disturb each other? Talk about rules relating to boyfriends and girlfriends. You don't want an extra roommate who isn't contributing his or her fair share. How will you resolve major disputes?

Helpful Hints

Looking for a rental unit can be fun or frustrating. If you plan your search ahead of time, use online sources to narrow your search and enlist an experienced parent or friend in the search, you will find the experience fun and not so frustrating.

Take your time. There are lots of details to think about. Comparison shop by looking at several units before making your choice.

To get the best feel of what it will be like to live there, visit the rental property during the day and at night, weekdays and weekends, if you can. Walk around the neighborhood.

Noisy neighbors are a common source of misery in an apartment or condominium. Try to find a place with concrete floors, walls that are well insulated and double-pane windows.

Exterior noise can also be a problem. I once lived near the emergency room of the county hospital and heard sirens frequently. I also lived next to a railroad's switching yards where the railroads were coupling and uncoupling box cars throughout the day! I only lasted there for four months.

If you are moving to a new city, you might start with a short-term rental (60 to 90 days) of a furnished apartment. Then, learn about your city and move to a more permanent place when you have a better feel for the city and where you should live.

For your first rental experience, do not spend a lot of money on furnishing the place until you get a good feel for whether you will be happy there or not. Rent furnishings initially. If you end up not liking the place, it will be easier and cheaper to move somewhere else if you haven't accumulated a lot of personal possessions.

Unlike buying a house or condominium, changing rental properties is not very expensive as long as you change at the end of your lease term. You don't want to leave early or break the terms of the lease.

Chapter 5: Arranging for Utilities

Besides paying your monthly rent and fees to your landlord, you will need to pay for some or all of the utilities that you use. The basic utility services are electricity, water and sewer. Some residence use natural gas to fuel the furnace, water heater and clothes dryer. Some residences use fuel oil or propane as the fuel for the furnace. Garbage pick-up and recycling services may also be provided by a separate supplier. Discuss with your landlord what is your responsibility.

Every residence will have an electricity provider. Normally, you, as the tenant, contact that supplier to start service. This can be done over the telephone or on the provider's website. There will usually be a small start-up or connection fee and security deposit. You will be charged for the electricity that you use. A meter on the residential property keeps track of your usage and is read by the utility company monthly. The service is billed monthly in arrears, that is, after you use the service and based on the actual amount used. Electricity will power your appliances, television, computer, lights and air conditioning. Heat may also be electric but also can be fueled by natural gas, heating oil or propane. Most heating systems use a furnace to create the heat. A blower forces the heated air around the residence. Other systems use a boiler to create steam that heats radiators in the residence. Your washing machine is electric. Your dryer may be electric or natural gas. Your water heater may be electric, natural gas, propane or fuel oil.

If you will be using natural gas, propane or heating oil, you need to contact the supplier for that service. Again, this can be done over the telephone or online at the provider's website. Like electricity, natural gas is billed monthly in arrears, based upon what you use. Heating oil and propane, a substitute for natural gas, is billed when delivered. These fuels are stored in fuel tanks on the property.

Water and sewer charges are usually paid by the landlord for apartments and condominiums. It is too expensive and difficult to separately meter each unit for billing purposes. The cost might be included in your rent. You need to ask the landlord.

Garbage pickup and recycling service is usually paid by the landlord. The cost might be included in your rent. You need to ask the landlord. Ask about how and when you need to take out your garbage. In high rise buildings, there is usually a garbage chute on each floor of the building that you put normal garbage items in. If you are renting a house, you will need to put out the garbage containers for pickup on a certain day of the week. Find out when and where you do that.

Utility providers usually make historical data on your residence available to you so you can accurately budget for the monthly cost. Many will provide you with a level monthly payment plan, created by dividing the annual cost by 12, so that you do not have large differences in payments from month to month. Paying these bills a few days late generally will not result in significant late payment fees. However, late payment may be reflected on your credit report and have a negative effect on your credit score. Not paying these bills for an extended period can result in shut off of the service.

Cable service used to be a normal part of every rental. Cable service provided you with access to television programs. Today, cable service can provide you with access to television stations, internet service and even telephone service. However, many people are now choosing to forego cable television service and subscribe to internet entertainment services instead. You can buy internet service separately. Major cell phone providers also can provide internet service to your rental unit. Broadband internet service may require a small satellite dish. The same is true of satellite "cable" providers. Your landlord may not allow you to install a satellite dish so ask the landlord before signing up for one of these services. Some apartment buildings and condominium buildings provide free internet service or may provide basic cable service. The cost is included in your rent or common area maintenance fee. There are various packages offered by these providers. You need to figure out what you can afford and what you want to pay for. Service quality may vary depending on the system used. Cable providers that have upgraded their systems to fiber optics can provide very high data download speeds and reliable service. Bad weather can impact services using satellite dishes.

The next chapter discusses cell phone services. You should think about cable, internet and cell service at the same time. There is a lot of competition for your dollars. You can save a lot of money by selecting the right package for your needs. Remember to use your budget in making your decisions.

Helpful Hints

The cost of utility services, other than cable, should be treated as a recurring expense in your budget. You have to pay whatever they charge you for the service.

You can control some utility costs by limiting your use. For example, you can keep your thermostat turned down to a lower temperature in the winter to save on heating costs and turned up to a higher temperature in the summer to save on air conditioning costs. You can buy and use a fan instead of air conditioning.

Cable services are offered in bundles. For example, television, internet and telephone services can be purchased individually, in pairs or all three services together. Within each service, bundles are also created. For example, you will be offered four or five choices of the television channels you can buy: 100, 200, 300 or 500 channels. Everything is designed to get you to buy and spend more. Therefore, consult your budget to determine how much you can spend and stick with that number.

In choosing cable, internet and telephone services, you will have to make sacrifices. Start out by meeting your basic needs. You can always upgrade later.

Bundles often require you to sign a service contract with a term of two or three years. Since your residence lease probably has only a one-year term, you should review the early termination provisions of your cable or internet service contract to understand what you may have to pay if you move.

Chapter 6: Choosing a Cell Phone and Service Plan

Everyone needs to have some way of receiving or placing telephone calls. Today, most people prefer a cell phone to a landline because you can carry a cell phone with you. There are dozens of choices in cell phones. The most elaborate cell phones, called smart phones, are telephones, cameras and portable mini-computers. The best smart phones can cost over a $1,000. A basic cell phone will send and receive voice telephone calls and text messages. These not-so-smart cell phones can cost under a $100. Providers will finance your purchase by including the cost in your monthly bill. Basic service can cost as little as $20 a month.

Besides the purchase of the cell phone itself, you will have to purchase a service plan. The plan may be prepaid, month-to-month or for one or more years. All plans provide for talk time and text messages. Often long distance calling within the United States is the same cost as local calling. International calls, however, may add to the cost. The cost of talk and text services is relatively small compared to the cost of the data plan portion of the service. The data plan supports the data transmissions used by the mini-computer. Data can be transmitted over the cellular network (most costly) or over Wi-Fi when you have a Wi-Fi signal available from another source, that is, an internet service provider.

In deciding what cell phone and service plan to buy, consider how you will be using the cell phone and then try to match those uses with the lowest cost plan. As previously mentioned, in determining your needs, you should also consider what needs will be met by your cable service. You should also consider whether many of your needs can be satisfied by purchasing a computer for your residence. If you cannot afford both a home computer and a smart phone, you should look very hard at what the advantages of a home computer are compared to a smart phone. A computer can be used as a work tool, a home budgeting and management tool, a research platform for buying goods and services, and an

31

entertainment center. While a smart phone can do many of these things too, the small size of the smart phone screen and keyboard make it more difficult to use and enjoy. Consider whether you really need to be carrying a high-powered mini-computer with you everywhere you go. Maintenance and repairs can be expensive. A mobile device tends to get damaged much more often than a home computer. Also note the differences in operating systems. Most PCs and MacBooks store files in a different way and location than smart phones and tablets. If you are used to working with a computer, you may not like the way a smart phone or tablet manages your files. A smart phone or tablet may not allow you to easily access files created on a computer.

In making your choices, you should do thorough research. Independent nonprofit rating companies, such as, Consumer Reports, should be consulted to avoid making serious mistakes and financial commitments. Because the products and services are constantly changing, I cannot make recommendations in this Guidebook. Do your research and shop around. Take your time. For the short term, you can purchase a cheap, prepaid cell phone to use while you do your shopping.

Helpful Hints

Start out by meeting your basic needs. You can always upgrade later.

Start with a basic cell phone ($100 to 200) and a low-cost laptop computer ($400 to 700). You can finance your purchases to get a low monthly payment that is within your budget.

Start with a basic service plan ($20) for talk, text and data. Include internet service in your basic cable plan. Once you have gained more experience about what your needs are and what you can afford, then you can consider upgrading.

If you are planning on traveling outside of the U.S. or take a cruise, contact your cell phone service provider before your trip to find out the cost of service outside of the U.S. Many tourists have been unpleasantly surprised to find out their cell phone usage on their trips cost hundreds of dollars extra.

Chapter 7: Transportation Choices

Another major decision you will need to make in your life is whether you should own and use a motor vehicle. If you live in a big city, you have several choices as to how you will get to work, run your errands, travel and visit your friends and family. Your city may have a subway, commuter rail or other fixed rail system. Your city may have an extensive bus system. Taxicabs and Uber®-like services may be widely available. Hourly rental car services may be available. Home delivery for groceries and other household needs may be cheap and widely available so you do not have to drive to the store. All of these services provide viable and much cheaper alternatives to owning and using your own motor vehicle.

If you do not live in a big city, you may have a bus system, taxicabs and Uber®-like services, but availability and proximity of these services are likely very limited. Delivery services may be available but usually at a high cost. Thus, owning and using your own vehicle may be your only reasonable alternative.

In selecting the location of your residence, consider your transportation choice. If you will use public transportation, you should live within walking distance to a station or stop for such public transportation. You will want to live fairly close to your workplace to minimize trip costs and time. Couples may have to compromise, with one using public transportation and the other using the only family car.

Owning your own motor vehicle is the most expensive form of transportation. You have the cost of the vehicle, gas, maintenance, repairs and insurance. The cost of parking, both at your residence and at work, must also be considered. Personal property taxes and licensing fees levied by state and local governments annually on the value of your vehicle can be substantial in big cities as these governmental entities try to discourage use of personal vehicles. In contrast, the cost of public transportation is usually subsidized by the government to make it more affordable to the users. Monthly use passes often provide substantial discounts from single use fares. Employers will often subsidize the cost of public transportation for their employees, particularly if the employer is located close to a station or stop.

Many people use several means of transportation. For day-to-day commuting to work, they may use public transportation. After work hours, they may use their own cars. This combination reduces commuting costs and avoids expensive parking fees at their work sites.

You are probably thinking that there is no way that you will use public transportation. But, if you are in a big city, it can work for you. It worked for me. I lived in Arlington, Virginia for a few years and worked in Washington, D.C., near the White House. Although I had owned a car for decades, I began to use the Metro and was pleasantly surprised at how much easier it was to use it for commuting instead of driving. My employer also provided shuttle bus service between offices in the area that was convenient and easy to use. I had my groceries delivered every week. After a few months in Virginia, I sold my car. When I needed a car, I rented a car by the hour, which I picked up from a parking area a few blocks from my apartment. If it can work for me, it can work for you.

Helpful Hints

If you are in a big city and live and work close to public transportation, then use it. You will save a lot of money that you can put into your savings and investment program.

If you buy a motor vehicle, buy a motor vehicle that meets your basic needs. Focus on the initial cost of the vehicle and its operating cost. If you will only use it for an hour or two each day, do not spend a lot of your budget on the motor vehicle.

Chapter 8: Credit, Borrowing, Leasing Alternative and Credit Cards

Previous chapters have discussed how to budget your expenses so your monthly earnings pay all of your monthly bills. This chapter discusses how you can use credit, that is, borrow or lease, to pay for goods and services that you do not currently have the money to purchase. You may have heard that credit is bad and you should never borrow. However, when properly used, credit can improve and enhance your life. It is only when improperly used that credit can be very damaging to you. Poor credit management can result in the loss of your residence, your car and even your ability to pay for food and clothing. Thus, you have to use credit cautiously and not incur too much debt for your level of income.

Banks, savings banks and credit unions extend credit to their customers. In the simplest transaction, you tell the banker how much you want to borrow and, if approved, you sign a "promissory note" payable to the bank and you will be given the money. This transaction is called a "loan". You are called the "borrower" or "debtor". The banker is your "lender" or "creditor". You will pay back the money over time, in one or more payments called "installments". You will also pay interest on the amount borrowed. "Interest" is calculated as a percentage of the amount outstanding over a certain time period. There may also be other fees you must pay, such as, an application or processing fee.

Your lender may ask you to provide property to secure the promissory note that you signed. This property is called "collateral". If you do not pay the promissory note on time, the bank can take the property away from you and sell it to pay the promissory note. If the property is real estate, in addition to the promissory note, you sign a mortgage or deed of trust that gives the banker a lien on the real property to secure the promissory note. The mortgage or deed of trust is recorded in the county real estate records so that everyone knows the banker has a lien on your real property. If the property is personal property, other than a vehicle, you sign a security agreement and financing statement that gives the banker a lien on the personal property to secure the promissory note. The financing statement is filed with your state's Secretary of State so that everyone knows the banker has a lien on your personal property. If the property is a vehicle, trailer, boat or other property that is titled by the government, you sign a security agreement and a document to record the lien on the title to the vehicle. The title will be given to you, but the banker's lien will be shown on the title.

When you borrow from a bank, savings bank and credit union, they will analyze your ability to pay back the loan on time. They will not approve the loan if they do not think you can pay back the loan on time. The cost of the loan to you, that is, the interest rate charged, varies depending on the type of loan, the collateral and your credit history or FICO® score. If you have a great credit history or score, the interest rate on your loan will be lower than someone with a poor credit history or FICO® score. Lenders compete with each other for your business by offering different interest rates, so you can save money by shopping around. As a general rule, credit unions offer the lowest interest rates on loans to their customers. One exception to that rule may be your car dealer. If you apply to finance the purchase of your car, the dealer will seek financing for you at very competitive rates or may offer you low-interest rate financing through a lender affiliated with the car manufacturer as an incentive to purchase that manufacturer's car.

Loans can also be made to you by other businesses. Your furniture or electronics store may lend you money to buy goods from them. Loans can also be made by finance companies, check cashers and payday lenders. College students can borrow from the government or their college.

Instead of purchasing a motor vehicle or other types of personal property, such as, furniture, and financing the purchase, you should consider leasing the motor vehicle or other personal property as an alternative. If you are leasing your vehicle, you choose the term of the lease, usually three to five years, and the dealer will provide you with the monthly lease payment. Leases generally include a maximum annual mileage allowance. If you exceed that allowance, you will have to pay extra charges per mile at the end of the term. You will also have to pay for any damage to the vehicle over normal wear and tear. When the lease term is over, the dealer owns the vehicle, not you. You will, however, have the option to purchase the vehicle at the residual value at the end of the term of the lease. The residual value is set at the beginning of the lease and is the dealer's estimate of what the value of the vehicle will be at the end of the term of the lease. The dealer determines the amount of the payments by subtracting the residual value from the purchase price to determine the amount it is financing. The dealer then applies an interest rate to that net amount over the term of the lease to calculate your monthly payment. The mileage allowance and damage clause are included in the lease to protect the dealer from unexpected declines in the residual value.

Lease payments are always lower than loan payments on a vehicle. That does not mean a lease is always a better deal. The payments are lower because, in a lease deal, you do not own the vehicle at the end of the lease. The loan payments include the total cost of vehicle so that you own it when your loan is paid off. As a general rule of thumb, if you plan on trading your new vehicle in every 3 or 4 years, a lease is probably a better form of financing for you. If you plan on keeping your vehicle for more than 5 years, a loan is probably a better way for you to finance your purchase.

Once you are satisfied with the lease terms, you sign a lease and are given possession of the vehicle. You are not purchasing the vehicle so you will not receive a title to the vehicle. Although you do not technically own the vehicle, you still get all of the benefits of the manufacturer's warranty. The manufacturer will pay for all major repairs during the warranty period.

Other personal property leases, such as, a furniture lease, are handled generally in the same way as motor vehicle leases. You get possession of the personal property during the term of the lease and a right to purchase the property at the residual value at the end of the lease. The length of the term of a personal property lease is usually much shorter than a motor vehicle lease. If you only need the furniture for a few months, leasing can make a great deal of sense. Delivery and pick up costs must also be considered as a part of the cost of the leasing personal property.

Most loans related to the purchase of consumer goods or services, other than vehicles, occur when the purchaser uses his or her credit card to pay for the goods. When you buy things using a credit card, the issuer of the credit card is making a loan to you. The proceeds of your loan are sent to the merchant who sold you the goods. Credit cards are a quick and easy way to pay for consumer goods or services. Payment of your credit card bill is normally due within 25 days after you receive the monthly credit card statement. If you pay the total amount due, that is, the "outstanding balance", you are not charged any interest for your short-term borrowing. If you do not pay the outstanding balance, then you will be charged interest calculated from the date of purchase. The interest will continue to be charged on the outstanding balance, including any new purchases, until you pay the entire balance outstanding. This is one of the most expensive types of credit. Interest rates of 36% annually or 3% <u>monthly</u> are common. In comparison, the interest rate on a mortgage loan on your residence or a car loan currently is in the range of 3 to 4% <u>annually</u>. Because of the high interest rate charged, you should always pay off your credit card balance each month if you can.

Some people are confused by what the cards they carry are. Most look alike, but some are credit cards, some are debit cards and some are ATM cards. When you use a credit card, you are borrowing money from the issuer of the card. The issuer is the bank or other company whose name appears on the card. The issuer sends you the monthly statement. You make your payment to the issuer. Visa® and MasterCard® are not issuers. These companies manage the network over which the information about your credit card is transmitted and payments are made from the issuer to the merchant, that is, the seller of the goods or services to you. Your debit card is issued to you by the bank where you have your checking account. When you use your debit card to buy goods or services, the transaction information is transmitted over a network to your bank and money is taken out of your checking account and transmitted to pay the merchant. You generally have to enter a personal identification number (PIN) at the merchant location to authorize a debit card transaction. That transmission may occur online at the time of your transaction or may occur offline in which case transmission of your transaction information occurs later. Your ATM card is issued to you by the bank where you have your checking account. It is used to get money out of the ATMs, that is, automated teller machines, at your bank and other locations that utilize the network(s) your bank participates in. These transactions are always online, always require you to enter your PIN and money is immediately deducted from your checking account. Fees are generally charged when you use an ATM other than one that is owned by your bank. A debit card can often be used as an ATM card too so your bank may issue you a combined debit and ATM card.

Credit cards are a great way to manage your cash flow and avoid overdrafts on your checking account since the money is not withdrawn from your checking account until you pay the bill each month. That will only happen once a month and only when you pay the bill. Using a debit card frequently can result in inadvertent overdrafts. People often lose track of how much they have spent. A spouse may not be aware of transactions made by the other spouse on the same day. Since debit card transactions may be approved offline, you cannot depend on your bank to reject, that is, not authorize, transactions that overdraw your checking account. It can be a very unpleasant surprise to find out your $3 cup of coffee resulted in a $35 overdraft charge! Because of the frequency with which inadvertent overdrafts occur for debit card users, I do not recommend using your debit card. Carry cash for small purchases. Use a credit card for large purchases, such as your groceries, but always pay off the balance each month.

Credit cards also provide you with greater consumer rights than debit cards do. For example, if you make an online purchase with a credit card and the seller does not send you the goods, you can contact your credit card issuer and the issuer will not charge you for the purchase. In contrast, if you make an online purchase with a debit card and the seller does not send you the goods, you cannot contact your bank and get your money back. In a debit card transaction, you have to get the refund from the seller. While credit and debit cards physically look the same to you, different laws and regulations govern credit card transactions and debit card transactions. The credit card laws and regulations were developed based upon the law and rules surrounding the making of consumer loans. The debit card laws and regulations were developed based upon the laws and rules applicable to paper checks. In addition, in credit card transactions, there are extensive contractual relationships between the card issuer, the merchant processor (a middleman who signs up the merchant and processes the transaction) and the merchant. The merchant pays a significant fee, often as high as 3% of the transaction amount, which is split between the card issuer and the merchant processor. On the other hand, when you buy something with a debit card, you are in essence giving the seller an electronic check. The merchant pays only a few cents to process each transaction.

Most credit cards also come with several extra benefits designed to encourage you to make your purchases with credit cards. Many credit cards now offer 1 or 2% cash back on purchases. Other typical benefits include extended warranty protection, protection against loss or breakage in first few months after a purchase, travel insurance for airline ticket purchases and damage deductible coverage when renting a car. Card issuers can provide these benefits because they make significant amounts from credit card transaction fees and from the interest paid by cardholders who do not pay off the outstanding balance each month. These benefits are not available to debit card users because transaction fees are low and no interest is paid by the cardholder.

When properly used, credit can improve and enhance your life. Use it cautiously and be careful not to borrow more than you can repay from your income.

Limit your use of your debit card. For many, debit card use is the cause of inadvertent overdrafts. Instead, pay for small purchases with cash.

Use your credit card as a cash flow tool. It prevents inadvertent overdrafts because you control when it is paid.

Use your credit card for online purchases. You will then be protected if the merchant fails to deliver the goods.

Be careful that you do not spend too much on your credit card. Studies show that using a credit card may result in people purchasing more at a store than they would if pay with cash.

Always, always pay your credit card off each month. If you cannot pay off the credit card balance each month, then stop using your card before you bury yourself in debt and interest charges you cannot pay back.

Chapter 9: Saving

After you have paid all your monthly bills, bought your groceries, paid off your credit cards and made your monthly loan payments, any money you have left is for discretionary spending. You can use it to buy more things or pay for entertainment. You should also save a portion of the money.

Your initial savings should stay in your checking account until you have built up a reasonable cushion in your checking account to ensure that you won't have an overdraft. This cushion will help avoid late fees on bills by ensuring that you always have funds to pay your bills in a timely manner. Maintaining a cushion in your checking account will also make it easier and less stressful to manage your monthly cash flow.

Once you have built up an adequate cushion in your checking account, you should open a savings account at the financial institution where you have your checking account. By opening a separate account at the same institution, you are earmarking the funds in your savings account for specific purposes. By separating the funds from your checking account, you are more likely to save and not spend those funds. By keeping the funds at the same institution, you may get credit from that institution for having that account and it may reward you in the form of reduce fees on your checking account. In addition, many institutions can link the checking account with the savings account to provide you with a low-fee overdraft protection program. Your savings account will also earn a small amount of interest.

Opening a new account is easy. You can do it in-person or online. The financial institution will have a basic savings account. This account will pay you a small amount of interest and you can withdraw your money at any time. You make deposits in the same way you do for your checking account. You can also transfer money from your checking account to your savings account in-person or online. To withdraw money, you can withdraw cash in-person at the financial institution location or you can transfer money from your savings account to your checking account.

As an alternative to a savings account, your financial institution may offer you a special kind of savings account called a "certificate of deposit" or "CD". The name of the account reflects its history. Originally, when you purchased this account, the financial institution would give you a piece of paper designated as a "certificate of deposit". You kept the "certificate" in a safe place and, when it was time to cash it in, you brought the certificate into the financial institution to redeem for your money plus interest. Now, since all the records are electronic, you don't actually get a certificate. You just get a new account number. The difference between a certificate of deposit account and a savings account is that, when you purchase a certificate of deposit account, you agree not to withdraw your money for a certain period of time, usually 3 months, 6 months, one year or more. In return for your commitment, the financial institution pays you a slightly higher rate of interest. If you withdraw your money before the committed date, which is called the "maturity date", you will be charged an "early withdrawal penalty", which usually is the loss of 3 to 6 months of the interest that you earned.

Try to put a small amount into this savings account each month until you build the balance up to a level equal to at least three-months' expenses. This account is your rainy day fund. It is used to pay unexpected expenses, such as, a dental bill or replacement of a flat tire. It is also a reserve you can draw upon if you lose your job. In addition, it can be used as a cash flow fund if you move. You can use these funds to pay the new landlord while you wait for your money back from the old landlord. The funds from the old lease should go back into the savings account.

If you are living paycheck-to-paycheck, you may find it difficult to save, but every little bit helps build up the fund. In addition, there are two times a year when most people have a chance to save. First, employers generally give a year-end bonus, which may be small, but nevertheless can be saved. Second, most people receive a tax refund in March or April. That money should go into savings. Remember, however, that having an outstanding balance on a credit card is extremely expensive. Pay those balances off first before put money in a savings account. Funds in your saving account should also be used to pay off a credit card balance if the funds in your checking account are inadequate. It is always better to use the money in the savings account rather than pay the high interest charges on credit card balances. Then, build up your savings again.

Helpful Hints

Saving is your first step away from living paycheck-to-paycheck.

While many financial institutions encourage you to open a savings account when you open your checking account, you should wait. Build up an adequate cushion in your checking account before you open a savings account. It is easier to manage one account rather than two and having only one account will reduce the chance of overdrafts.

When you do open your savings account, pat yourself on the back as a reward for making a big step in good financial management.

Chapter 10: Investing

Once you have built up your rainy-day fund in a savings account to the level described above, then you can start investing. Investing has two purposes. One purpose is to create a fund for your retirement. After you retire, your invested funds will replace your earnings from your job. A second purpose is to generate additional income for you. Your investments will grow in value and pay interest and dividends.

Most people begin their investment program by making a contribution out of each paycheck to their employers' retirement plan. Usually, the retirement plan is called a "401(k) plan", in reference to the section of the Internal Revenue Code that excludes your contributions to the plan from your gross income for income tax purposes. If you work for a nonprofit, such as a school, hospital or religious organization, the retirement plan is called a 403(b) plan, but the tax treatment is the same. This means that, when you report your wages on your income tax return, your retirement contributions are deducted from your wages before the income tax is computed. In addition to reducing your income taxes in the year of your contribution, no income taxes are payable with respect to investments within the plan as long as the money remains in the retirement account. You can buy and sell investments and receive interest and dividends on your investments without paying income taxes on those earnings.

Payment of income taxes is deferred until you make withdrawals. Income taxes are payable on withdrawals from your retirement account at ordinary income tax rates. The total amount withdrawn is considered as taxable income to you. A 10% penalty may also be assessed for withdrawals prior to retirement age. However, there are several hardship exemptions to those penalties. Money can be withdrawn without penalty for medical expenses, a down payment on your first house, up to 12 months of college expenses, burial expenses, foreclosure or eviction expenses and casualty losses. You can also borrow up to 50% of your funds, without penalty, if certain conditions exist.

Many employers match employee contributions to his or her retirement account up to a certain percentage of the employee's salary, usually 2 to 5%. Matches vary, but often 100% matching is provided by the employer. A "100% match" means that, for every dollar you put in to the account, your employer will put a dollar in. Although your employer is making a payment for your benefit, you do not pay income taxes on the employer contribution until you withdraw the funds from your retirement account.

You should try to maximize your contributions to take full advantage of your employer's matching program. If your employer has a 100% matching program, your immediate investment return is 100%. Plus, you double your future earnings because you earn on twice as much money. Your employer's matching contribution may be subject to a vesting period. That means you cannot withdraw the employer's matching contribution until a certain period of time has elapsed. In addition, if your employment is terminated prior to the end of the vesting period, the employer may take back its contribution to your account.

Contributing to your retirement plan is just one of the steps required to finalize your investment. Once you have funds in the account, you must choose where your money will be invested from a list of 10 to 15 investments that have been chosen by your employer. To understand what these investments are, you need to learn a few basic investment terms: mutual fund, stock and bond.

A "mutual fund" consist of a pool of investments managed by an investment advisor. The pool is segregated, that is, held separate, from other assets of the manager, and the assets are usually held in a business trust. The investor buys shares in the mutual fund that represent an undivided interest in the assets of the pool. Mutual funds can invest in various things, but retirement plans only invest in mutual funds that hold stocks and bonds. Mutual funds are priced at the end of each trading day. When you buy a share of a mutual fund, your purchase does not occur until the end of the trading day when the value of a share is determined. Sales of shares of a mutual fund are handled at the same time. As the value of the mutual fund's investments goes up or down, the value of the investor's share in that pool goes up or down. The investor also receives his or her share of the dividends or interest received by the pool as well as gains or losses on investments sold. The manager of the mutual fund will charge a fee for its services, which is expressed as a percentage of the total assets of the mutual fund.

"Stock" is a type of investment. Stock is issued by a corporation and represents an ownership interest in the corporation. When you own stock, you own a small percentage of the corporation. Two types of stock are "common stock" and "preferred stock". The individual interests in common and preferred stock are referred to as "shares". The owners are referred to a "stockholders" or "shareholders". Most investors invest in common stock. A corporation distributes its earnings in the form of "dividends". Dividends paid on preferred stock are usually paid at a fixed rate each year and payment is made before (preferred) payment of dividends to the common stockholders. Although stockholders are the owners of the corporation, stockholders have no liability for payment of the corporation's debts and liabilities. However, if a corporation stops doing business and sells off all of its assets to pay its debts and liabilities, creditors, including claims of employees, are paid first. The stockholders are the last to be paid. Preferred stockholders are paid before common stockholders.

The value of common stock rises and falls based upon several factors, the most important of which are the ability of the corporation to generate "sales" of its products and services and "net income" or "earnings". In basic terms, net income and earnings are the amounts left when you subtract the total expenses of the corporation from the total income the corporation receives from sales of its goods and services during a certain period. Income can also be generated by selling assets for more than the purchase price of such assets. These are referred to as "capital gains". The value of common stock also depends on what people expect the corporation to earn in the future. The value of common stock depends on how much others desire to own the common stock, too. Some common stocks are more popular than others. In addition, the value of common stock depends on economic conditions in general. If the economy is doing well, corporations usually do well, people have more money to invest and stock prices tend to go up. Economic downturns normally result in a decrease in common stock values. The impact of the economy on common stock values is one of the main reasons why you should invest for the long term. Over the short term, the values will go up and down, but, historically, over the long term, values have gone up. Of course, no one can guarantee what will happen in the future and corporations do fail from time to time.

In addition to issuing stock, corporations also issue debt. This debt is issued in the form of "bonds". Governments also issue bonds. The bonds issued by the United States are considered a very safe investment. The safety of bonds issued by a corporation depends on the corporation's creditworthiness. The issuers of bonds pay interest periodically on the principal amount of the bonds. The interest paid on bonds issued by states and municipalities is not subject to Federal income tax. These bonds are referred to as "tax-cxcmpt" bonds.

The list of investments for employer-sponsored retirement plans are fairly standard. Typically, you will be offered what are called "target retirement" funds. These funds determine the mix of stock and bond investments on the assumption that all investors will retire in a certain year. For example, there may three target retirement funds offered. One fund assumes retirement in 2040, another in 2050 and another in 2060. You pick the fund closest to your retirement year. If the target retirement date is far away, the mix includes mostly stocks. When target retirement date is near, the mix includes a higher percentage of bonds. The funds are managed this way because, as a general rule, stock values fluctuate more widely than bond values. As people get closer to retirement, they want more stable values because they need to be able to withdraw a certain amount each year to live on. Besides target retirement funds, you will also be offered funds that invest entirely in stocks as well as funds that invest entirely in bonds. Stock funds offered are usually "large cap", "medium cap" and "small cap" funds. These designations refer to U.S. companies with different market capitalizations or total market values. In simple terms, market capitalization is determined by multiplying the number of shares of stock outstanding times the market value of an individual share. For example, on March 26, 2021, Apple Inc. had 16.8 billion shares of stock outstanding. The market value of each share was $120.40. Its market capitalization was $2.02 trillion (16.8 billion times $120.40). Large cap companies are the largest companies in the U.S., like Apple and Amazon. A large cap fund only invests in the stock of the largest companies. A small cap fund only invests in the stock of the smallest companies that are listed on the U.S. stock markets. A mid cap fund invests in the stock of medium-sized businesses that are neither large cap nor small cap. You may also be offered a "global stock" fund. Unlike a large cap fund, which invests only in U.S. companies, this fund invests in large cap stocks but the companies can by headquartered around the globe.

The bond funds you will be offered in employer-sponsored retirement funds will be designated by the length of the average maturity of the bonds that the fund holds. Thus, you will be offered short-term, medium-term and long-term funds. All of the funds will invest in high quality bonds, that is, bonds where the issuers have high credit ratings. All of the funds will invest in bonds that have a fixed interest rate, that is, the interest rate on the bond is the same throughout the term of the bond. As a general rule, the long-term funds provide highest interest rate returns and the short-term funds provide the lowest interest rate returns. Also, as a general rule, the value of long-term funds will fluctuate more widely than the value of short-term funds. Among other things, fixed-rate bond values fluctuate based upon changes in market interest rates. Because the bonds held by these mutual funds have fixed interest rates, as interest rates go up, the bonds become less desirable and bond values go down. As interest rates go down, bond values go up. Because your income in an employer-sponsored retirement plan is already tax deferred, the bond funds offered in such plans do not invest in "tax-exempt" bonds.

As a beginner with many years until retirement, you should choose a fund that invests in U.S. large cap stocks. These are stocks issued by the largest companies in the U.S. and are considered very low risk investments. While the value of these stocks will vary as the market goes up or down, over the long term, the value of these stocks should increase because the companies' earnings and assets should grow each year. If any company owned by the fund starts performing poorly, the fund manager will sell shares owned in that company and buy shares in another company that has better performance.

If you are uncertain what to do about your employer-sponsored contributions and investments when you start a job, your employer should allow you to start your contributions later, at the beginning of any pay period. There is no special enrollment time period, like there is with health insurance. The plan manager should also allow you to change your investments at any time. A website may be provided where you can research the mutual funds and make and change your choices.

Other major tax-sheltered retirement investment alternatives are individual retirement accounts (IRA) and Roth individual retirement accounts (Roth IRA). If you are covered by an employer-sponsored retirement plan you cannot contribute to an IRA, but you can contribute to a Roth IRA up to the annual contribution limits, currently $6,000. An IRA or Roth IRA can be opened at a bank, savings bank, credit union or brokerage firm. The types of investments that you can make in an IRA or Roth IRA are much broader than with employer-sponsored retirement plans. The investments generally include any investment product offered by the institution holding your account.

Your contributions to an IRA are deducted from your gross income in the tax year the contribution is made. This lowers your taxable income. This is not an itemized deduction so you reduce your taxable income whether or not you itemize or use a standard deduction to determine your taxable income. Capital gains, dividends and interest earned on your IRA are tax deferred. No income taxes are paid until you withdraw money from your IRA. All withdrawals, however, are taxed at ordinary income rates. As with employer-sponsored retirement plans, withdrawals made before retirement age (currently 59.5 years) are subject to a 10% penalty unless you qualify for a hardship exemption. Hardship exemptions include qualified higher education expenses for you and your family members, up to $10,000 for a first-time home purchase, qualified medical expenses, and expenses due to unemployment.

Your contributions to a Roth IRA are not tax deductible. Capital gains, dividends and interest earned on your Roth IRA, however, are tax exempt if withdrawn after retirement age. After retirement age, no taxes are paid when you withdraw money from your Roth IRA. Early withdrawals, however, are taxed at ordinary income rates but only on the portion of the withdrawal that represents earnings, that is, capital gains, dividends and interest. Your contributions can be withdrawn at any time without income tax or penalties. Withdrawals of earnings made before retirement age (currently 59.5 years) are subject to a 10% penalty unless you qualify for a hardship exemption. Hardship exemptions include qualified higher education expenses for you and your family members, up to $10,000 for a first-time home purchase, qualified medical expenses, and expenses due to unemployment.

If you do not have an employer-sponsored retirement plan, you can open either an IRA or Roth IRA. Neither an IRA nor a Roth IRA has clear tax advantage. What is best for you depends on whether you think your income tax rate when you make a withdrawal at retirement will be higher than your income tax rate when you make your contributions. If you are currently in one of the lowest tax brackets, the tax deductibility of your contributions may only save you only 15% of the contributed amount. That 15%

is locked up in the IRA and provides a bigger base upon which you earn. For example, if you contribute $2,000 to your IRA, you save $300 on your taxes that year. Your IRA investment, however, is $2,000. If you are in your early 20s and assuming a 4% interest rate, compounded annually, your $2,000 should be worth at least 5 times your investment or $10,000 when you reach retirement age. If you withdraw $10,000 at retirement age and pay the same income tax rate, you will owe taxes of 15% or $1,500. Your net withdrawal will be $8,500. If, instead of an IRA, you invest the net amount of $1,700 in a Roth IRA, your $1,700 should be worth at least 5 times your investment or $8,500 when you reach retirement age. When you withdraw $8,500, you will owe no taxes on that amount. This example assumes that your tax rate remains the same when you contribute the money and when you withdraw the money. In such a case, the Roth IRA is probably a better choice because you can always withdraw your contributions without penalty. If you withdraw early from an IRA, you may have to pay a 10% penalty. If you expect your tax rate to be higher when you retire, a Roth IRA is also a better choice. It is only when you expect your income tax rate to be lower at retirement that the IRA is a better choice. Since most of us are in a lower tax bracket at the beginning of our careers, then the Roth IRA is likely the best choice overall. Notwithstanding the foregoing, your employer-sponsored retirement plan with matching contributions is always the best choice for you because of the matching contribution.

Once you have established your checking account, a savings account and a retirement account, then the funds remaining after paying all your bills and paying for all the other necessities of life should go into one or more general investment accounts. The main purpose of these investment accounts is to generate additional income for you. While there are thousands of investments to choose from, there are only a few basic types that you should start with as the foundation of your investment plan. Making these basic investment does not require you to perform an in-depth analysis of a corporation's financial statements. That is left to professionals.

With a general understanding of the investment terminology and how the markets work, you can select reasonably safe and secure investments that should return you a reasonable rate of return over the long term.

To begin, you need to learn a few more investment terms. A "broker" is an individual who is licensed by a federal agency, the Securities and Exchange Commission, to buy and sell investments for other people. Brokers are usually licensed by the state where they work too.

A "brokerage firm" is the company where brokers work and where you go to open an investment account. Brokerage firms may have physical locations and an online presence.

"Exchange traded funds" (ETFs) and "index funds" are forms of mutual funds with certain important differences. Generally, these funds are passively managed. That means that the fund's investment manager is not analyzing the individual stocks or bonds for quality or performance. The manager is simply investing in the stocks or bonds that make up a particular index. For example, there is an index called the "S&P 500" index. The "S&P" refers to "Standard & Poor's" which is a private rating agency. The "500" refers to the 500 largest U.S.-based publicly-traded corporations. The index consists of the aggregate market capitalization of the common stocks of those 500 corporations at any point in time divided by a proprietary divisor created by S&P. The components of the index, that is, the stocks included in the index, are updated quarterly. The manager of a S&P 500 Index fund will invest in the shares of those 500 corporations in the same proportions as the stocks are included in the index and will also adjust those holdings quarterly as companies are added and deleted from the index. The manager has no discretion to make any other investments. The price of ETFs changes throughout the day in the same manner as stocks. When you buy shares of an ETF, your trade happens right away. You do not have to wait until the end of the trading day as you do with index funds.

An "exchange" is a market place where stocks and bonds are traded on each business day during certain hours.

When you buy or sell stocks or bonds, you enter your trades through your broker. You cannot trade directly on an exchange. Trades can be handled in person, over the telephone or online. You contact your broker by one of these means and tell the broker what you want to do. If you are buying, the broker will want to see funds in your investment account to pay for the purchase. Trades usually settle, that is, you pay or receive the money, two or three business days after you enter the trade. Brokerage firms will extend credit to their customers and the credit is secured by the investments. "Margin" is the money you borrow from a brokerage firm to purchase investments. When you sell an investment, a brokerage firm will often allow you to buy other investments with the proceeds of that sale right away. The firm won't make you wait for final settlement of the initial "sell" trade.

Mutual funds transactions are made with the investment manager of the fund. You can do this through your broker or you can set up an account directly with the investment manager. ETF and index fund trades are handled in the same manner as stocks and bonds. The trades are made through your broker.

The fees paid to brokers have gone down significantly in recent years. Many online brokerage firms offer no-fee trades on stocks and reduced or no fees on bonds and certain mutual funds. If you invest directly with a mutual fund manager, you may save the fee that your broker would charge you. Mutual funds also have an investment management fee. This fee is expressed as a percentage of the assets of the fund, usually around 1 or 1.5 percent. ETFs and index funds also have an investment management fee, but, since the fund is passively managed, the fee is significantly lower than a normal mutual fund fee. The ETF and index fund fee may be as low as .2 percent. Mutual funds may also have an early redemption fee. This fee is paid when you sell your mutual fund shares before the expiration of a certain holding period. This redemption fee is to encourage you to invest for the long term. Some mutual funds prohibit frequent short term trading. If you buy and sell your shares too often, the fund may prohibit you from purchasing new shares.

You set up your general investment accounts at a brokerage firm. Brokerage firms may have physical locations as well as an online presence. As with opening a checking account, you should only establish your account at a place that offers the basic services you need: buying and selling stocks, bonds, mutual funds and ETFs.

In making your choice, cost should be a major consideration. Focus on several cost components. First, consider the cost to maintain the account. This is usually in the form of a monthly service charge. Providers will often waive this charge if you meet certain requirements, such as, maintaining a certain amount of money in your account at all times. Next, consider transaction and commission charges. There may be fees for each buy and sell transaction made from the account. These charges will vary based upon the type of investment you are trading in so you need to focus on the transaction and commission charges for those investments.

As with checking accounts, competition for your business is fierce. If you have a good paying job and have had no financial difficulties in the past, you should be able to find a suitable investment account free of regular monthly charges and have low transaction and commission charges.

Safety of your money on deposit is also another consideration. Your investment accounts at a brokerage firm should be insured by the SPIC. "SPIC" stands for Securities Protection Investor Corporation. SPIC is a nonprofit corporation that insures accounts held at brokerage firms up to $500,000. Your IRA and Roth IRA accounts are separately insured from your personal investment account. Like FDIC insurance of bank accounts, the insurance applies when the brokerage firm goes bankrupt.

Convenience and ease of use is another important consideration. Unlike banks, savings banks and credit unions, brokerage firms have few physically locations where you can go to deposit your money, make withdrawals and talk to your broker. Therefore, you should select a brokerage firm that has an easy to use website and smart phone application. Several fintechs, such as Cash App and Robinhood, offer applications that are directed at first-time investors and are easy to use and understand. Many of the brokerage firms are affiliated with a bank that can provide you with checking account services. If you feel ready to move to a new level of money management, that is, you don't require in-person service from your bank anymore, you should consider moving your checking account to the bank affiliated with the brokerage firm that you choose.

Once you have your investment account established at a brokerage firm, you need to choose your investments. As a beginner investor, you should avoid selecting individual stocks or bonds. You do not have the expertise to make those choices. You should rely on the professionals to make those choices.

Many financial advisors suggest that beginner investors should invest in a S&P 500 ETF or index fund or a similar well-established index fund. Over the last 10 years, the return on the S&P 500 index has averaged over 10% per year. With long-term interest rates on safe investments currently below 3 or 4%, such a return is reasonable. The S&P 500 index includes all of the best U.S.-based corporations. The top S&P 500 top five holdings as of March 1, 2021, were Apple, Inc., Microsoft, Inc., Amazon.com Inc., Facebook Inc. and Alphabet Inc. (Google) and represented about 10% of the Index.

As you build up your investment knowledge, you can look at investing in more focused mutual or index funds. There are thousands to choose from. As a short cut to analyzing a lot of funds, look at the choices your employer provided you for its retirement plan. Use those choices as a basis for expanding your personal investment choices. At least annually, compare the performance of those alternative choices to the performance of your S&P index fund. If the alternatives are performing significantly better, then allocate more of your future investment dollars to those funds. If the alternatives are performing significantly worse, then you may want to sell your shares in those funds and put your money back into your S&P index fund.

At least annually, you will be paid dividends and interest that the funds receive on the stocks and bonds held by the funds. Capital gains will also be distributed. You will be required to report those income amounts on your annual income tax returns. If you own a mutual fund that invests in tax-exempt bonds, the fund will distribute those tax-exempt earnings to you at least annually. You do not include tax-exempt interest on your Federal tax return but those earnings may be taxed by the state you reside in. Capital gains realized on the sale of tax-exempt bonds are taxable.

Helpful Hints

Invest on a regular basis. The market goes up and down throughout the year. By investing on a regular basis, you can smooth out the effects of those fluctuations. Sometimes you will buy at the low, sometimes at the high.

Stick to your long term investment strategy. Don't panic when the market suddenly goes down. People who sell during a panic usually miss the market rebound. Those people end up buying back into the market at higher prices. Normally, it is best just to ride out the cycles.

Don't buy a stock based on the tip you heard at work. Professionals track and analyze stocks on a regular basis and will have acted on positive information long before that information reaches you.

Don't buy cryptocurrencies, like bitcoin. Cryptocurrencies are highly speculative investments and are too difficult for a beginner to analyze properly.

Don't jump on the bandwagon when everyone is buying into a stock. You will pay too much for a stock that is extremely popular. Through a regular investment program in an S&P 500 index fund, you will be buying the stocks of all the best US-based corporations and increasing those investments quarterly as the index components are rebalanced by S&P.

Don't be a day trader. Day traders bet on the fluctuations of a stock within a day. It is impossible for you to make intelligent investment choices within one day. Despite the stories that you hear of people making a living by day trading, most day traders lose money.

Chapter 11: Buying a Car

Chapter 7 discussed the factors you should consider in deciding whether you should buy a car or other motor vehicle for transportation. Assuming you have decided to buy, this chapter discusses the buying process and using credit to buy a vehicle.

The purchase of a car or other vehicle is a complicated and time consuming process. You have to decide what type of vehicle you want and what best meets your needs. Do you need a car, truck or van? Do you need a compact car or SUV? Do you want a new or used vehicle? What brand and model do you want? What is the most economical, safest, and most reliable? Do you want a gas, hybrid or electric vehicle?

Buying can also be a lot of fun, if you do your homework and are not afraid to say "no" to the salespeople. A good way to start the process is by looking at the recommendations of independent rating companies. Consumer Reports, which is a nonprofit corporation that tests and rates all kinds of consumer goods, including vehicles, is a good place to start. It provides ratings of the best new cars and the best used cars by year. It evaluates various factors from performance to safety. Its ratings discuss the pros and cons of the vehicles. Use the recommendations to educate yourself on what is available, how much they cost and what will be best for you. Create a list of the top 5 vehicles you want to test.

Make sure the vehicles you select are within your budget. Remember to include insurance, maintenance and gas costs in determining what your selected vehicles will cost to own. Motor vehicle insurance, which is required under state law, can cost $150 to 250 a month. Insurance costs increase as the value of your vehicle increases so you pay less for a lower priced vehicle. Maintenance, including tires, can average $60 a month. New cars come with four or five year warranties. The car manufacturer pays for all maintenance and repairs except ordinary maintenance, that is, oil changes, and tire wear. For an average driver, gas can cost $200 to 250 a month or $.15 to $.18 a mile. A fuel efficient car can save you up to half those amounts. An electric car charged away from home costs around $.10 to .12 a mile. If charged at home, the cost may be half that amount plus the cost of the charger if you have to pay for it. In addition, remember to add the sales tax your state charges on top of your agreed purchase price. Sales tax is payable upfront and equals 6 to 8% of the purchase price of the vehicle. If you are in a high personal property tax state, like Virginia, you should also factor in the annual license and personal property tax payable. It can be over a thousand dollars per year. The average licensing fees are around $600 a year or $50 a month. Monthly parking fees should also be considered.

Let's add up all of these costs to see if you really can afford that vehicle. Let's assume you select a vehicle with a purchase price of $25,000, the dealer adds a $1000 preparation fee and your sales taxes are 6%, then the total purchase price is $27,560. You make a $1,000 down payment and get a great interest rate of 3.2% on a loan with a 5-year term. Then, your monthly car payment will be $498. Add insurance at $150 a month, maintenance for a new car at $30 a month, gas at $200 a month and licensing fees at $50 a month. The total monthly cost is $928. If you lease instead, you can probably lower the monthly payment by $100 to 150, but you won't own the vehicle at the end of the lease. Consider whether you can still afford the vehicle you have chosen. If not, think about buying the new vehicle you have chosen but as a used car that is two or three years older.

Once you have chosen your top 5 and assuming you are still buying a new vehicle, go to the dealers that sell those vehicles and test drive the vehicles you like. Test them all so you can narrow your choices down to one or two vehicles. If you want to buy a used vehicle, go on the internet and search for the vehicles you like to find out what dealers have the vehicles in their inventory. Then, visit those dealers to test them and narrow your choices.

After you have narrowed down your choices to one or two vehicles, you have to agree on the price with the dealer. Some dealers have a fixed price and do not negotiate with you over that price. Other dealers will negotiate the price. Consumer Reports provides a service at a low price that tells you how much the dealer markups are on new vehicles. This helps you know what offer to make. Remember to include all the dealer fees in your offer. Many dealers will have a "preparation charge" of $1,000 that is in fact just part of the profit. Negotiate a total price excluding sales tax.

Once you have a price that you like, then negotiate the value of your trade, if you are trading in a used car that you own. Your state may offer an incentive to do a trade by deducting the value of your trade from the price of the new vehicle before applying the sales tax. If you do not like the trade value offered, have your car appraised by a used car buyer, such as, CarMax, to see if you can get a better deal. You can also check with a valuation service, such as Kelley Blue Book, to determine the approximate value.

Next, you focus on how you will pay for the car. Most people make a small down payment and finance the rest. Financing can be in the form of a loan secured by the car or in the form of a lease. If you get a loan secured by the car, you will decide the term of the loan. Four to five years is normal. The dealer will offer you various interest rates. The shortest term loan gets you the lowest rate. The dealer will tell you what your monthly payment will be under each scenario. The payment includes principal and interest only. Sales tax is included in the principal amount. Your monthly car payment does not include the cost of insurance, maintenance unless maintenance is included in the price of the vehicle or the annual car licensing fees. When you pay off the loan, you will own the vehicle free and clear. Assuming the payment is within your budget, then you proceed to sign the sales contract and financing documents. The dealer will transfer title to the vehicle to you. The title will show that the dealer has a lien on the vehicle. That lien will be released when you pay off the loan and your title will be updated to show the release.

If you are leasing your vehicle, you choose the term of the lease, usually three to five years, and the dealer will provide you with the monthly lease payment. Leases generally include a maximum annual mileage allowance. If you exceed that allowance, you will have to pay extra charges per mile at the end of the term. You will also have to pay for any damage to the vehicle over normal wear and tear. When the lease term is over, the dealer owns the vehicle, not you, but you will have the option to purchase the vehicle at the residual value. The residual value is set at the beginning of the lease and is the dealer's estimate of what the value of the vehicle will be at the end of the term. The dealer determines the amount of the payments by subtracting the residual value from the purchase price to determine the amount it is financing. The dealer then applies an interest rate to that net amount over the term of the lease to calculate your monthly payment. The mileage allowance and damage clause are included in the lease to protect the dealer from unexpected declines in the residual value.

Lease payments are always lower than loan payments on a vehicle. That does not mean a lease is always a better deal. The payments are lower because, in a lease deal, you do not own the vehicle at the end of the lease. The loan payments include the total cost of vehicle so that you own it when your loan is paid off. As a general rule of thumb, if you plan on trading your vehicle in every 3 or 4 years, a lease is probably a better form of financing for you. If you plan on keeping your vehicle for more than 5 years, a loan is probably a better way for you to finance your purchase.

Once you are satisfied with the lease terms, then you sign a lease. You are not purchasing the vehicle so you will not receive a title to the vehicle. Even though you do not technically own the vehicle, you still get the benefit of the manufacturer's warranty.

Helpful Hints

First-time car buyers usually underestimate what the cars they want will really cost them. As a result and within a few months after the purchase, first-time car buyers often find they have difficulty managing to live within their budgets.

You can save yourself thousands of dollars by purchasing a used car. A car's value drops by an average of 15 to 20% in the first year.

When purchasing a used car, you have to be diligent in finding a car that hasn't been in an accident or flood or had significant mechanical difficulties. Ethical and trustworthy used car dealers will provide you with an independent report to show you that the vehicle hasn't been in an accident or flood or had significant mechanical difficulties.

If you purchase a used car that is under three years old, the car should still be under the original manufacturer's warranty. This will protect you from unexpected major mechanical difficulties. In addition, most manufacturers will offer extended warranties to owners who purchase the extended warranty during the original warranty period. The extended warranty will cost $2,000 to 4,000, but it protects you from unexpected large mechanical bills later. If you purchase the extended warranty when you buy the used car, the cost of the extended warranty can be included in your loan amount.

I cannot overstate the importance of making sure that the used car you buy will not have major mechanical problems in the future. If the used car will not be covered by a good warranty plan, you should have the car thoroughly inspected and tested by a good mechanic before you buy. The mechanic can tell you what parts are wearing out and when replacement will likely be necessary. You need to factor those repair costs into your decision as to whether the used car is a good buy for you.

Most extended warranties are also transferable or the value of the unexpired term is refundable when you sell the car.

If you decide to buy an extended warranty, make sure that you are buying the manufacturer's extended warranty plan. Many large auto dealerships offer their own extended warranty plans that pay for your service only if you have the service done at that dealership's locations.

Gas is a big part of your monthly cost. To help you keep within budget, consider carpooling or using public transportation occasionally if you have a long commute to work. Reducing the mileage you drive slows the decline in the vehicle's value and reduces maintenance costs.

Chapter 12: Buying a House or Condominium

Like renting an apartment, buying a house or condominium, your residence, is one of the biggest actions you will take in your life. It takes a huge amount of your budget, often 40% or more of your net earnings every month. Thus, you should spend a lot of time and effort in taking this action.

Home ownership is also a way to build your wealth. Homes and condominiums historically have increased in value over the long term. The Federal government encourages home ownership by facilitating a mortgage market that provides low interest rates and long term loans to buyers. The Federal government also allows you to treat the mortgage interest and real estate taxes that you pay as itemized deductions on your income tax return. In addition, the Federal government excludes the first $250,000 in gain that you realize when you sell your home from income and taxes any gain above that threshold at capital gains rates that are significantly lower than the rates you pay on ordinary income.

Let's refresh our memory of the terminology used. A "house" is a separate structure designed for one family to live in. If it is designed for two families to live in separately, it is called a "duplex". A house consists of multiple rooms: a living room, kitchen, one or more bedrooms and bathrooms. The house may be one or two stories, with or without a basement, and with or without a garage. With a house, you normally own the yard surrounding the house. A "townhouse" is usually at least two stories with the side walls attached to the adjacent townhouses. Each townhouse is individually owned with a commonly owned association to handle maintenance and repairs to common elements.

A "condominium" (condo) usually looks like an apartment. The ownership structure, however, is different from an apartment. Each condominium in a building may have a different owner. The building itself, the walls, the lobby and other common areas, are owned by a condominium association, which in turn is owned partially by each of the condominium owners. In contrast to an apartment building, where every unit is rented, a condominium building includes units where the owner lives as well as units that have been rented to others. In some cities, you also have what are called "coops" or "cooperative housing". In a coop, the building is owned by a cooperative association which is owned by all the resident of the building. The individual living spaces are purchased by individual owners, much like with a condominium, but the ownership structure is in the form of a perpetual lease.

When you buy your residence, the initial document you will be required to sign is called a purchase and sale agreement (the "Purchase Agreement"). The Purchase Agreement is the legal agreement that specifies what you are buying, how much you will pay, that is, the purchase price, how you will finance the purchase, what the conditions to closing are and what happens if you do not do what you promise. You are called the "purchaser" or "buyer". The person or company that you buy from is called the "seller". The printed terms in a Purchase Agreement are usually set forth on a standard form approved by the local real estate commission or realtors' association. Most states have a residential real estate law that imposes certain minimum duties that the seller has to every purchaser. These requirements are primarily in the form of disclosure requirements.

You finance your purchase with bank, savings bank, credit union or other mortgage lender. Your debt is evidenced by a promissory note that sets forth the amount borrowed, the interest rate, the term of the loan, and the monthly payment. The loan is secured by the residence. You sign a mortgage or deed of trust to provide your lender with a lien on your residence. The mortgage or deed of trust is recorded in the county's real estate records. The term of a loan may extend out as long as 30 years.

Use your budget to determine how much you can afford for a monthly loan payment. A rule of thumb is 30 to 40% of your net earnings. Include in your payment amount all of the recurring fees that you will charged by the lender, such as a monthly amount to pay for property insurance and real estate taxes. Do not include utility costs for electric, gas, cable, water and sewer. Determine how you will pay the upfront down payment. The down payment is usually 5 to 20% of the purchase price. If you put less than 20% down, your lender will probably require you to purchase "private mortgage insurance" or "PMI". PMI protects the lender if you stop making your payments. If you do not qualify for a conventional loan, you may qualify for a special program sponsored by the Federal Housing Administration (FHA). These loans are called "FHA Loans". In this program, you pay a fee to the FHA to insure you loan instead of getting PMI. In addition, if you are a veteran, you may qualify for a special mortgage loan program run by the Department of Veterans Affairs (VA) that allows you to put zero dollars down when you purchase your house.

Estimate other amounts that you will need upfront to buy your residence, such as security deposits for utilities, utility installation charges, furnishings, dishes, pots and pans and bedding. Remember to include moving costs if you have to pay someone to move you. Save up money to pay those upfront amounts or arrange to borrow the money from someone.

Once you have arranged the funds to pay the upfront costs, you can begin your search for a residence that is within your budget. You start by contacting a real estate broker that works in the area where you want to buy. Real estate brokers are normally paid by the seller when a sale occurs so don't worry about paying the broker you choose. Real estate brokers are licensed by the state in which they work. Under state law, the real estate broker will explain to you upfront and in writing his or her relationship with you and how he or she is paid. Normally, you are not required to sign an agreement with a real estate broker although the real estate broker may require you to sign a statement indicating that you understand the disclosures that the broker has made to you.

After contacting a real estate broker, you explain to the broker what you are looking for and the broker will conduct a search for properties that meet your needs. Most real estate brokers have access to properties listed for sale in an online system called the "multi-list" system. There are also online services, such as Zillow and Trulia, that provide similar information. A real estate broker can help you find the right residence. The real estate broker will also help you through the buying process by giving you guidance on market prices, by drafting the Purchase Agreement, by helping you find financing and by helping you through the steps to close the transaction. The broker will normally ask you to pre-qualify for a mortgage loan sufficient to purchase a residence in your price range. The broker will help you through this pre-qualification process. When a sale occurs, your real estate broker will be well compensated by the seller, usually 2.4% of the purchase price, so do not be afraid to use a lot of your real estate broker's time and expertise. However, once you start working with a real estate broker, as a courtesy to that person, you should continue working with him or her. It is also important to stick with your broker to avoid conflicts between brokers over commissions. For example, if you look at a house with one broker and then use a different broker to look at the house again, the first and second broker may both claim part of the commission if you ultimately buy the house.

The most common way that a residential real estate transaction occurs is with both the purchaser and seller represented by real estate brokers. When a seller wants to sell the seller's residence, they sign a "listing agreement" with a real estate broker. The broker appraises the property to determine at what price it should be listed for sale. The listing agreement provides that the broker will market the property for the seller. The listing agreement provides that the seller will pay the real estate broker a commission, usually 6% of the purchase price, when the property sells. The seller's broker lists the property on an online system available to brokers in the area, which is called the "multi-list" system. As part of that multi-list process, the seller's broker offers to pay a broker representing the purchaser 40% of the broker's commission when a sale is closed.

After you locate a property that you like, your broker will prepare a Purchase Agreement. The Purchase Agreement contains several parts. In the Purchase Agreement, you offer to buy the property from the seller at a specified price on a specified date if all the conditions of your offer are met. As part of the offer, you make an "earnest money" deposit with the seller's broker to show your good faith and to provide funds the seller may keep if you default under the terms of the Purchase Agreement. The Purchase Agreement outlines the terms of the loan that you intend to obtain to make the purchase, including the amount of the down payment you will make. The Purchase Agreement will specify how and when you will make an inspection of the physical condition of the property and how inspection issues will be resolved. Normally, the buyer hires an inspector for $300 or 500 to perform the inspection and provide a report. The Purchase Agreement will specify how title to the property will be examined and insured. Normally, the seller will arrange for a title insurance company to send you a title commitment that explains who has title and any exceptions to title that are noted. The seller pays for title insurance. You will pay separately for title insurance for your lender. The Purchase Agreement will set forth the timeline to complete or close the transaction. In the normal form of Purchase Agreement, if the purchaser defaults, the only damages that the purchaser pays is the loss of the earnest money deposit. On the other hand, if the seller defaults, the purchaser can force the seller to comply and complete the transaction or pay damages to the purchaser. Some forms of Purchase Agreements do not limit the purchaser's liability to loss of the earnest money deposit. Therefore, you should make clear to your real estate broker that you want your offer to be limited to loss of the earnest money deposit.

After your broker completes the Purchase Agreement with the terms of your offer, you sign the Purchase Agreement and your broker delivers the Purchase Agreement to the seller's broker. The seller then has a few days to respond in writing by accepting the offer, rejecting the offer or making a counteroffer. If a counteroffer is made, you have a few days to respond in writing by accepting the counteroffer, rejecting the counteroffer or making a new counteroffer. This exchange of writings continues until an offer is accepted or the parties stop making counteroffers. Any oral communications occur between the brokers. Normally, you and seller do not meet to discuss or negotiate the Purchase Agreement.

Most people do not involve an attorney before the Purchase Agreement is signed. This happens for several reasons. First, because the real estate industry has standardized the form of the Purchase Agreements, the brokers can explain them to the purchasers and sellers. Second, buyers often are worried about the cost of using an attorney, particularly when many offers are rejected. The problem with this custom is that, once the Purchase Agreement is signed, it binds the purchaser and seller. If there is a problem, it must be resolved under the terms of the Purchase Agreement. An attorney representing a buyer before the Purchase Agreement is signed may choose a form or add certain language that is more favorable to the purchaser if a problem occurs later.

If you do not hire an attorney before you offer is accepted, you should hire an attorney when the offer is accepted. Because most documents used in residential real estate transactions are on standardized forms, most real estate attorneys will handle a simple residential transaction for as little as $500. The attorney can also help you through financing, inspection, title issues and closing matters. For example, few purchasers or brokers know how to read a title commitment, understand what constitutes a significant title issue and how to fix title issues. An attorney helps fill that gap in knowledge. Often, the lender is relied on to protect the purchaser from title defects. Such reliance, however, does not give the purchaser a remedy against the lender if the lender makes a mistake. The attorney also reviews the Settlement Statement. The Settlement Statement sets forth the amounts paid by the purchaser and seller, who is paid and where the funds for closing come from. This information comes from the Purchase Agreement, the loan documents, the title commitment and county real estate records. Mistakes are common because the person preparing the Settlement Statement, usually a person at the title company who is closing the transaction, has to rely on others to provide him or her with the correct information. Your attorney can verify from all of the documents and other sources that the information is correct.

Once the Purchase Agreement signed, you formally apply to a lender for the financing and provide the documentation required by the lender. The lender will verify your income, assets and liabilities. The lender will hire an appraiser to determine that the market value of the property equals or exceeds the purchase price. You will have to pay a nonrefundable application fee and appraiser's fee. The lender will provide you with a "good faith estimate", which is required by law and discloses to you in writing the lender's fees, costs and expenses associated with the loan that you have requested. Normally, you will also ask the lender to "lock in" the interest rate the lender has quoted to you. This "lock in" agreement binds the lender to provide you with that interest rate, if you qualify for the loan and close the transaction within the time period set forth in the agreement. Under the terms of the Purchase Agreement, the lender has a certain amount of time to approve you for the loan. If you are not approved, you can normally cancel the Purchase Agreement without penalty.

You will also hire an inspector and proceed through the inspection process. It is common for there to be several problems detected in the inspection process. Working through your broker, you try to resolve those problems either by the seller correcting the problems before the closing or by the seller paying you money at the closing so you can correct the problems. If these problems cannot be resolved within a specified time period, you can normally cancel the Purchase Agreement without penalty.

The seller provides the purchaser with a title commitment. The purchaser reviews it and provides a copy to the lender. As part of the title and loan process, a surveyor is hired to prepare a survey of the property showing the boundary lines and location of all the improvements, that is, the structures. This survey is to determine that the house you are buying is on seller's property and not on the neighbor's property. It also will show if any of the neighbors' structures are on the seller's property. The survey will show if

71

utilities have rights of way on your property where no structures can be located. If the property is covered by a homeowner's association, you will also review documents related to that association as part of either the inspection process or the title process. These documents may include a declaration of covenants and restrictions, articles of incorporation and bylaws of the association, the association's financial statements and the association's reserve study. The reserve study lists the common elements that the association is responsible for maintaining, repairing and replacing and shows whether the association has the funds to pay the costs associated therewith. Having an attorney to help you with this process can be very helpful. If the association owns and operates several common elements, such as, a swimming pool or clubhouse, or employs several people, such as a property manager and maintenance staff, you want to make sure that the association is operating on a financially sound basis. You want to make sure that current association fees are adequate to pay current expenses and that reserves have been created to repair and replace the common elements as they wear out. The association may have incurred debt to pay for common improvements. You want to make sure the debt can be paid out of the current fees. Associations have the power to raise their monthly fees and make special assessments against the property owners in order to pay for association expenses. You do not want to buy into a property when you might face a significant increase in monthly fees or a large special assessment. If the development you are buying into is new, there may be litigation between the developer and the association related to defects in construction or the failure of the developer to provide promised amenities. You do not want to buy a property that is in litigation. Problems are resolved through the brokers. If no resolution can be found within the time limits set forth in the Purchase Agreement, you can normally cancel the Purchase Agreement without penalty. Note, however, if you cancel at this point, you will be out-of-pocket for certain expenses, such as, your loan application fee, the appraiser's fee, the inspector's fee and your attorney's fees. The title company does not earn its fees unless you close the transaction.

If the financing is approved, inspection issues are resolved and title and survey issues are resolved, then the parties proceed to complete the transaction at the closing. In most cases, the parties meet at a specified location and time. In addition to the purchaser and seller, the closing will include their attorneys, their brokers, representatives of the lender and representatives of the title company. At the closing, the parties will give final approval of Settlement Statement that details what the purchaser pays for and what the seller pay for. The Settlement Statement shows what funds the lender provides and its fees and charges. It also shows how much money will be paid to each broker and the title company. It will list any other fees, including the closer's fee, taxes due and recording costs. Real estate taxes due on the property will be prorated between the buyer and seller based on the closing date. The purchaser will sign numerous documents from its lender, including a promissory note and mortgage or deed of trust. The seller delivers a warranty deed conveying the property to you. The seller will be paid the net amount due to the seller per the Settlement Statement. The brokers will be paid their respective share of the commission. The seller gives the purchaser possession and the keys to the property. After the closing, you will receive the recorded warranty deed and a title insurance policy issued by the title company.

In many states, rather than closing the transaction in person, you close in "escrow". Under this procedure, a person or entity is designated as the escrow agent. This person is often the seller's attorney or the title company. You sign an agreement with the escrow agent that instructs the escrow agent to close the transaction when certain conditions are met. The seller and your lender also sign agreements with the escrow agent instructing the escrow agent to close the transaction when certain conditions are met. You sign the documents required in the transaction and send them to the escrow agent. The seller and the lender also sign the documents required in the documents and send them to the escrow agent. You send the money you are required to pay to close the transaction to the escrow agent. Your lender sends the loan proceeds to the escrow agent. When the escrow agent has all of the signed documents and the funds required from you and your lender, the escrow agent will close the transactions. Copies of the signed documents will be delivered to you, the seller and your lender. The escrow agent disburses the funds to the seller, the brokers, the title company and any others who need to be paid. The escrow agent records the warranty deed and the mortgage or deed of trust.

There are a few differences between the purchase of a house and a condominium or coop. With a condominium and coop, the condominium or coop association will usually require the purchaser to apply for approval to purchase the condominium or coop. This may involve a background and credit check. If you are not approved, you cannot complete the purchase. The association documents are a much more critical part of the purchase decision. The documents may contain significant restrictions on your use and renovation of the condominium or coop. Monthly association fees may also be substantial, particularly if the association has full-time employees, numerous common elements to maintain, such as a swimming pool, gym or clubhouse, and has incurred debt to pay for improvements.

You will need to arrange for utility services for your residence in the same manner as you do when renting. Try to coordinate the change of service with the seller through your brokers. In addition, you need to obtain property or homeowner's insurance. Your lender will require that it be listed as a co-insured on your insurance policy. Insurance is discussed in more detail in the next chapter.

To help you be a more educated purchaser, I want to discuss common problems that arise in residential real estate transactions and how those problems can be addressed.

Often, your lender's appraisal of the property comes in below the purchase price in the Purchase Agreement. This means that the lender will only lend you the promised percentage of the appraised value rather than the full amount of the loan that you had applied for. If this is a conventional loan, you can make up the difference by increasing your down payment. You can also ask the seller to lower the purchase price to the appraised value, but the seller has no obligation to do so. Finally, you can cancel the transaction in which event you will get your earnest money deposit back.

Unexpected liens on the property are another common problem. Sometimes the seller has a judgment lien against him or her that has been recorded. In such a case, the lien must be released before you can close on the property. Sometimes, these liens are against someone with a name similar to the seller. In such case, the seller needs to convince the title company that the lien is not against the seller. This can often be done with an affidavit from the seller.

Fences encroachments against the neighbor's property are another common problem. A fence encroachment exists when the seller's fence has been built partially on the neighbor's property. To resolve this title issue, the seller should try to enter into a written agreement with the neighbor to allow the fence to remain in its present location. If that is not possible, then you can ask the seller to relocate the portions of the fence that encroach on the neighbor's property to remove the encroachment. You can also cancel the transaction in which event you will get your earnest money deposit back.

Sometimes, the neighbor's fence or garage encroaches on the seller's property. If allowed to continue, the seller could lose its rights in the portion of the property where the encroachment exists. To avoid permanently losing this land, the seller could enter into an agreement allowing the encroachment while the structure exists. The seller can also ask the neighbor to move the structure. If the seller cannot resolve the problem to your satisfaction, you can cancel the transaction in which event you will get your earnest money deposit back.

Another common problem occurs when the seller or its predecessor builds an addition to the house or garage without getting a permit from the local building department to build the addition or garage. To resolve this problem, you should require the seller to get the project approved retroactively. If the seller does not want to do that, you can cancel the transaction in which event you will get your earnest money deposit back. If you proceed with the purchase without requiring correction of this problem, you assume the risk that you will have to pay to have the project permitted and approved yourself.

Building structures or planting trees on a utility easement are another common problem. In many communities, the utility companies will have the right to locate poles and cables under and along certain portions of residential properties. Usually, these rights of way or easements run along the front or back lot lines. Under the terms of these easements, lot owners are prohibited from building on property burdened by the easements. In addition, if trees or bushes are planted within the easement, the utility company can cut down and remove the trees and bushes. The survey prepared in connection with your purchase will identify where the easements are and whether any structures are built on the burdened property. It will not locate trees or bushes. If a structure encroaches on the easement, your lender and you should require correction of the situation. To correct the situation, the seller will have to obtain the utility's written agreement to relocate the easement or reduce the size of the easement. If the utility will not agree, you can cancel the transaction in which event you will get your earnest money deposit back.

Various inspection problems can occur. Some may be very serious, such as, the discovery of asbestos that needs to be removed, and need to be corrected before the closing. Others are minor, like a leaky faucet, do not need to be corrected immediately. In addition to asbestos, common major issues are discovery of mold, termites, lead paint, radon gas in the basement and foundation damage or deterioration. As a first-time homeowner, you probably should cancel the transaction if you find any major problems. If you decide to proceed with the purchase, you need to make sure that the problems are fixed by qualified professionals.

Many inspection problems relate to things that wear out over time, like water heaters, air conditioners and the shingles on the roof. When confronted with these issues, you need to determine whether you will have the money to replace those items when the inspector says that replacement will be necessary. You can ask the seller to replace items nearing the end of their useful life. If you cannot afford to replace the items noted and the seller is unwilling to pay for the replacements, then you can cancel the transaction in which event you will get your earnest money deposit back.

Helpful Hints

When you are ready to buy, the first step is to find a good, experienced real estate broker. Ask your family members, friends and colleagues at work for recommendations. If you know the area where you want to live, drive around that area and make a list of the brokers who have "for sale" signs in that area. The brokers with the most sales listings will probably be the best real estate brokers in that area.

Going to open houses is not a good way to search for your home. Work with a good, experienced real estate broker to refine your search online before you start visiting properties. Note also that open houses are often used by newer brokers to find clients. If you go to an open house and provide the broker with your name and contact information, you will probably get solicited for the broker's business.

When you are ready to make an offer, you should also find a good attorney who has a lot of experience doing residential real estate transactions. Your broker can probably give you some referrals to experienced attorneys. Meet with that attorney to discuss your needs and the attorney's involvement in your transaction and the fees. The first consultation is usually free and the attorney can give you guidance on when you should bring the attorney into your transaction.

If you are in a real estate market that is extremely competitive, you will be pressured to make decisions quickly. As a beginner, you need to resist those pressures and only moved forward when you feel comfortable with the transaction. Having an attorney available to look after your interests can help you a lot in resisting the urge to make decisions too quickly. You may lose out of a house because you didn't act quickly enough, but that house may have been fraught with problems. You may have avoided those problems by not acting too quickly.

Don't let this Chapter discourage you from purchasing a house. I intended only to give you a brief overview of the process so that you know what steps are involved in the transaction. Looking for a house can be a lot of fun. Enjoy it. Let the professionals, your broker, attorney, inspector and appraiser, worry about the details. Listen to the professionals' advice and act in accordance with their recommendations.

Chapter 13: Buying Insurance to Protect Yourself

Any successful money management plan can quickly fall apart in the face of common events of life, such as, your sickness or the loss of your job. Uncommon events of life, such as car accidents and natural disasters (tornadoes, floods, earthquakes and hurricanes), can also wreak havoc on your financial planning. To protect yourself, you should carry adequate insurance. In some cases, minimum insurance coverage is mandated by law. In other cases, your lender may require you to carry insurance to protect it from loss in the event of damage to or destruction of its collateral. In other cases, while you are not required to carry such insurance, it makes financial sense to do so.

All U.S. citizens and resident aliens are required by Federal law to carry health insurance. Currently, there is no financial penalty or fine, however, for a person's failure to do so. The Federal government and your state government are the insurer of people living on an income near or below the poverty level through the Medicaid program. People over the age of 65 and those with long term disabilities are insured through the Federal government's Medicare program. Veterans may qualify for coverage from the Veteran's Administration, which has its own network of hospitals and doctors. Many people obtain private insurance through their employer who usually pays most of the employee's premiums. Everyone else should purchase insurance through their state marketplace or the Federal marketplace, healthcare.gov. No one can be denied coverage. Your pre-existing medical conditions cannot be considered by insurers when selling you a policy. The Federal government provides financial subsidies for many people to purchase private health insurance under the provisions of the Affordable Care Act. For many people, health insurance purchased under the provisions of the Affordable Care Act may be premium free because of the Federal subsidies.

79

You should purchase health insurance through the channel that applies to you. Health insurance pays for routine healthcare and also for major healthcare costs, such as, hospital stays and surgery. Policies generally have a deductible that must be paid by the insured before the insurer begins payments. Policies purchased under the Affordable Care Act must pay for 100% of the cost of certain preventative healthcare services, such as, wellness checkups, preventative screenings and vaccinations, and the deductible does not apply to those services. Most policies also require the insured to make a co-payment for each visit to a doctor or specialist.

If you own a motor vehicle, your state's laws require you to purchase minimum levels of motor vehicle liability insurance. Liability insurance pays claims filed against you by people who have been injured or who have had their property damaged in an accident in which you are involved. If you are at fault in an accident, you are responsible for any claims above the liability limits. If you finance the purchase of or lease your motor vehicle, your lender or lessor will require that you also purchase collision and comprehensive insurance to cover damage to or theft of your vehicle. Collision insurance pays for damages to your motor vehicle in the event of an accident. Comprehensive insurance pays for damages to your motor vehicle from causes other than an accident, such as, hail or a tree limb falling on your motor vehicle. Comprehensive insurance also pays you for the value of your vehicle if it is stolen. These policies have a deductible that you pay before the insurer pays. You may select different deductibles for liability, collision and comprehensive coverages. The higher the deductible the lower your premium will be. Whether you are required by law or by your lender to carry motor vehicle insurance, it makes financial sense to carry motor vehicle insurance. You should discuss with your insurer's agent the appropriate limits for liability coverage that make sense and are affordable to you. In addition, you should carry uninsured motorist coverage. This insurance pays for injuries to you and your passengers when the person who caused the accident has no or inadequate insurance. Most insurers also provide towing coverage for a nominal annual charge.

Motor vehicle insurance is sold by people authorized by the insurance companies to sell policies for them. These people are called "insurance agents". In addition, to being appointed by the insurance companies, insurance agents are licensed and regulated by the state that they work in. Some insurance agents only sell policies issued by one company, such as, Allstate or State Farm. These agents are known as "exclusive" or "captive" agents. Other agents, who are called "independent" agents, sell for multiple insurance companies. Independent agents, however, do not sell policies issued by insurance companies with exclusive agents, such as Allstate and State Farm. When selecting an insurer, an independent agent can give you price quotes from several insurance companies. If you want a quote from Allstate, State Farm or another insurer with exclusive agents, however, you have to contact one of its exclusive agents.

It pays to shop around for motor vehicle insurance. The industry is competitive and premiums can vary significantly from one insurance company to the next. In addition, you should periodically obtain new quotes from other companies to make sure the insurance company that you initially selected remains the best buy. Cost is not the only factor to consider in selecting an insurance company. You should also consider how the insurance company handles its claims. The largest insurance companies have a very streamlined process for handling claims. Smaller companies may be more difficult to deal with if you have a claim.

Motor vehicle insurance policies are generally written with terms of no more than one year. Many have a term of only six months. The premium is due upfront, that is, when you purchase the policy, but most insurance companies will allow you to pay the premium in monthly installments, which installments will include an interest charge for deferring payment.

The amount of future premiums due on renewal of your policy will be affected by several factors. Premiums may go up if you receive a traffic ticket for a moving violation or if you are involved in an accident. Some insurance companies consider your credit score in determining what your premium will be. So, if your credit score goes down, you may face a premium increase when renewing your policy. Premiums may also increase for reasons that have nothing to do with you, such as the insurance company has experienced a high volume of claims from other drivers in the area where you live.

If you have financed your motor vehicle, your lender will require that it be listed either as an "additional insured" or a "loss payee" on your policy. This means that, if a claim is being paid to you, your lender will need to approve how much of the payment will go to you and how much of the payment will go to the lender. It also means that the lender will be notified if you fail to make your premium payments or if the insurance policy is canceled for some reason.

If you finance the purchase of your home or condominium, your lender will require you to purchase property and casualty insurance covering damage to your home or condominium from certain causes, most commonly, fire. This insurance will also provide you with coverage of your personal property in your home or condominium. It also protects you from loss in the event claims are asserted against you that are related to the property, such as, someone slipping and falling on your property. Whether you are required by law or lender to carry property and casualty insurance, it makes financial sense to do so. Your residence represents a major investment and you should protect yourself from loss if something happens. Damages from wind (hurricanes), floods, and earthquakes are usually not covered by a basic property and casualty insurance policy. You have to pay your insurer extra for those coverages or obtain that coverage from another insurer. If you are in an area prone to hurricanes, such as Florida, coverage may be difficult to obtain, very expensive and carry high deductibles. The State of

Florida has a state-sponsored insurance company to provide wind insurance to those who cannot otherwise obtain coverage from a private company. Flood insurance is only provided by the Federal government under the National Flood Insurance Program, which is managed by the Federal Emergency Management Agency. Premiums vary based upon the risk assumed by the insurer. Those in areas prone to flooding pay higher premiums. Earthquake insurance is available through private property and casualty insurance companies. Not every company will offer this coverage. Those that do provide coverage may have high premiums and high deductibles.

Home and condominium insurance policies generally have a one-year term. Payment is due upfront, but most insurance companies will allow you to make monthly payments with interest. Often, your mortgage lender will have you pay a portion of your monthly premium into an escrow account and your lender will use that money to pay the annual premium. As with motor vehicle insurance, your lender will require that it be listed as an "additional insured" or "loss payee" on the insurance policy.

If you are renting an apartment, house or condominium, your landlord may require you to carry liability insurance to cover damages that you may cause to the rental property or to others on the property. A condominium association may also require this coverage. Renter's liability insurance is included in a renter's property and casualty insurance policy. This policy will also cover damages to and loss of your personal property in the event of covered perils, such as fire or theft.

Beyond the coverages discussed above, most people assume they should have life insurance, which pays a fixed amount in the event of a person's death. However, you should only purchase life insurance if you have dependents who will need the money in the event of your death. When you purchase life insurance, you will maximize the protection for your dependents by buying a "term life" insurance policy because, for the same monthly premium, you can buy a higher death benefit than you can when buying other more expensive types of life insurance. This insurance is paid for on a monthly basis and is relatively cheap. Often term life insurance is provided or subsidize by your employer as an employee benefit. Term life insurance should pay regardless of how you die. Do not buy a policy that only pays in the event of accidental death. It won't pay if you die from cancer or other illness. Do not buy "whole life" insurance. This insurance combines life insurance with a tax sheltered savings program. It is expensive and agents selling it earn large commissions. In addition, do not buy a life insurance "annuity". This insurance combines life insurance with a tax-sheltered investment program. The benefit paid by a life insurance company to your beneficiaries when you die is not subject to Federal income taxes.

Before you determine what level of life insurance you can afford, you should purchase adequate disability insurance. To the extent you have money leftover in your budget to purchase life insurance, then you should spend those dollars on term life insurance.

Disability insurance pays you if you become disabled. The odds of you becoming disabled during your working career are much greater than the odds that you will die during your working career. Disability insurance is often offered by employers as an employee benefit. If your employer does not offer this benefit, personal disability insurance policies are relatively cheap if purchased when you are young and healthy. These policies automatically renew annually as long as you pay the premiums. Unlike employer-provided disability insurance, a personal policy will continue to cover you when you change jobs.

There is a major difference in the way employer-provided and personal disability policies are treated under Federal income tax law. When you make a claim, the payments you receive under an employer-provided disability policy is consider ordinary income for Federal tax purposes, but payments received under a personal policy are not subject to Federal income tax. If you pay a portion of the premiums for an employer-provided disability policy, the benefit payments you receive will be subject to Federal income tax to the extent attributable to the employer's payment of the premiums, but not taxable to the extent attributable to your payment of premiums. For example, if your employer pays 50% of the premiums for the employer-provided disability policies, 50% of the payments you receive when disabled will be taxed as ordinary income for Federal tax purposes.

Several important provisions in disability policies should be carefully examined. One provision involves the definition of when you are considered disabled. In most basic policies, you are only considered disabled if you cannot work at any job. For skilled or professional workers that definition of disability is inadequate. Skilled and professional workers need to purchase a policy that considers them disabled if they cannot perform their present jobs or if they suffer a substantial loss of income as a result of the disability, that is, partial disability.

Another important provision in disability insurance policies involves when the insurance begins to pay. Some policies referred to as short-term disability policies begin to pay within weeks after you stop working. Other policies referred to as long-term disability policies begin to pay three or more months after you stop working. In buying this insurance, you should always insure for the long-term disability because that is when you have the most financial exposure. Short-term events can be covered by your savings programs.

Many people think that they do not need disability insurance because of Federal Social Security disability insurance coverage. It is true that Social Security disability insurance provides some long-term coverage. There are several problems with the Social Security program, however, that should be considered. First, it is total disability insurance. You are not covered if you can perform any job. Second, it is long-term insurance. Coverage does not start until six months after you become disabled. Third, coverage is limited. Your monthly benefit payment will be equal to the amount you would receive as your Social Security full retirement benefit, which currently averages about $1,200 a month. Furthermore, the claim process can be difficult, take a long time and require litigation. There is a defined list of disabling conditions. If you have one of those conditions, like a spinal cord injury, your claim will likely be processed quickly with resolution with five or six months. Yes, five or six months is considered quickly. If you do not have one of those conditions, then your claim may take years to process and require you to hire a lawyer to pursue your claim. If you are successful and remain disabled for two consecutive years, you will also be enrolled in Medicare. Your Medicare coverage will require payment of certain premiums. Such coverage continues while you are disabled plus seven years after the end of your disability.

None of the insurance policies discussed above, with the exception of Medicaid, cover the cost of long-term healthcare in a nursing home or other facility. Some insurance companies offer long-term healthcare insurance but the premiums for coverage adequate for most people is unaffordable. As a result, you should try to cover this risk through your savings, investment and retirement plans and your disability insurance plan. For those who qualify for Social Security retirement benefits (age 62 and above), Social Security will continue to pay you while you are in a long-term healthcare facility.

With respect to the liability coverages that you get under your motor vehicle insurance policy and home or condominium insurance policy, you can buy extra liability coverage by purchasing an umbrella insurance policy. These policies are relatively affordable and provide additional coverage over and above what the underlying insurance policies cover.

Helpful Hints

A comprehensive insurance program is an important part of financial management.

Health insurance protects you against high medical bills if you have a serious illness or accident.

Motor vehicle insurance protects you against claims asserted by people who you may be involved in an accident with. It also protects the money that you have paid for the motor vehicle.

Home or condominium insurance protects the money that you have invested in your home or condominium, including amounts that you borrowed to purchase your home or condominium.

Disability insurance continues your income stream if you become disabled.

Life insurance provides funds to your dependents when you die.

You probably cannot afford to purchase full coverage in all of these areas. Try to allocate your budgeted premium dollars in a way that makes the most sense for your personal situation.

You can often save on premium costs if you buy your motor vehicle and home insurance from the same insurer.

Conclusion

Handling and managing your money are two of the most important things that you will do in your life. I hope this Guidebook has taught you the basic, practical things you need to know to properly handle and manage your money. Keep it as a guide to use and refer to as your financial matters get more complicated.

Made in the USA
Las Vegas, NV
29 November 2023

81812492R00049